CHARMING
SMALL HOTEL
GUIDES

AUSTRIA

CHARMING SMALL HOTEL GUIDES

AUSTRIA

Edited by Paul Wade and Kathy Arnold

DUNCAN PETERSEN

This edition published 1993 by
Duncan Petersen Publishing Ltd,
54 Milson Road, London W14 0LB,
and distributed by
Automobile Association Publishing, c/o Exel Logistics MS,
Invicta Warehouse, Sir Thomas Langley Road,
Medway City Estate, Rochester, Kent

Conceived, designed and produced by Duncan Petersen
Edited by Team Wade, The Chapter House, Chiswick Mall,
London W4 2PJ

Editors Paul Wade, Kathy Arnold
Assistant editor Joshua Dubin
Principal inspector Nicholas T. Parsons
Art director Mel Petersen

A CIP catalogue record for this book is available from the
British Library

ISBN 1 872576 13 3

Typeset by Midford Ltd, London
Originated by Reprocolor International S.R.I., Milan
Printed by G. Canale & C. SpA, Turin

Contents

Introduction

This is yet another addition to the well-established series of Charming Small Hotel Guides. After France, Italy, Spain, the British Isles and Germany, we focus on Austria. Its natural beauty, combined with its history and culture, makes it one of the most alluring tourist destinations.

To complete that idyllic experience, a charming, small, family-run hotel is essential. We have over 250 listed here, most with fewer than 30 rooms ranging from total luxury to rustic simplicity, from city to mountain-side, from lakeside to vineyard. All have a warmth of welcome, a desire to make guests comfortable and the willingness to go an extra step to please.

Entries
In this volume, as with Germany, our warmest recommendations are reflected in the full-page reports. Following these are shorter entries, four to a page. These are not 'second class' hotels, but for one reason or another do not justify a full page.

Bedrooms
Many of our readers prefer the comfort of their own separate bed and are keen to know about twin-bedded bedrooms. In most hotels, the traditional Austrian double bed is essentially two singles, pushed together, with separate mattresses and separate duvets. We found that a true 'double bed' was a rarity.

Public rooms
From the smallest tavern to the grandest castle hotel, the *Stube* is an essential ingredient. Usually wood-panelled, this room, with its bench seats, large tables and *Kachelofen* (ceramic stove) is the place to eat, drink and relax.

Meals
Breakfast is usually a buffet, an enterprising mixture of fresh and dried fruits, cereals, cold meats and cheeses with a variety of fresh rolls and breads. Eating in at night is an excellent way to meet both the host and other guests who stay on to chat in the *Stube* after dinner over a fiery glass of *Schnaps*.

Bio
Austria is an environmentally-aware nation. In hotels and restaurants, *Bio* indicates the use of wholefood or organic products. *Bio* rooms are furnished in natural materials, and some have master-switches that cut off all electric current during the night to ensure a natural night's sleep.

Introduction

Smoking
This is still a popular vice, with only a handful of hotels able to offer non-smoking dining areas or bedrooms.

Electricity
Few of the hotels listed have 'international' sockets, so adaptors are essential for visitors with electric razors.

Credit cards
Austrian hoteliers are fighting a battle with the major credit card companies over their charge rates. They prefer to take Eurocheques, travellers cheques, even cash.

Your host and hostess
Most inn-keepers enjoy being involved with their guests, whether it is cross-country skiing or hiking, tasting wines or teaching cookery. Pleasant as an overnight stay will be, a longer visit will always give added insight into the local family or region.

Travel facts
The staff at the Austrian National Tourist Offices around the world are particularly helpful to the individual traveller when it comes to special interest holidays. The Austrian National Tourist Office in Britain is at: 30, St. George Street, London, W1R 0AL. Tel: (071) 629 0461; fax: (071) 499 6038. In the United States it is at: 500 Fifth Avenue, Suite 2009-2022, New York, N.Y. 10110. Tel: (212) 944 6880; fax (212) 730 4568.

Flights
For U.K. residents, British Airways has a regular service to Vienna from both London Heathrow and London Gatwick, with three flights every day. For visitors to Vorarlberg in western Austria, it is more convenient to travel via Zurich in Switzerland. British Airways also has a regular service to Zurich from both London Heathrow and London Gatwick, with four flights every day.

Car hire
Budget Rent a Car have 16 outlets in Austria, including 6 airport locations. The rates for their Holiday Drive and Business Traveller programmes include local taxes, vehicle insurance and unlimited mileage, as well as CDW, personal accident insurance and one-way rentals at no extra charge.

How to find an entry
Entries are arranged geographically. Austria is divided into 5 regions; we start in Western Austria and move clockwise

Introduction

through North-western, North-eastern, Eastern and finally Southern Austria. Each of our regions consists of one or more of the nine Federal States that make up Austria.

Each state section follows a set sequence:

First comes an area introduction, with an overview of the hotel scene in that state, mentioning some hotels that were too big or too simple to be included in the full listings.

Then come the main, full-page entries for that state, listed in alphabetical order by town.

Finally come the shorter, quarter-page entries for that state, again listed in alphabetical order by town.

There are three easy ways to find a hotel:

Use the maps between pages 10 and 19. The numbers refer to the page in the book where a hotel is listed.

If you know the state you are visiting, browse through that section until you find a place that fits the bill.

Use the indexes which list entries both by place name (p187-191) and by hotel name (p183-186).

How to read an entry

At the top of the page is the area of Austria; below that is the name of the Federal State; then follows the type of hotel, its town and, finally, the hotel itself.

The snowflake   ❄

We have added the snowflake symbol to help you recognize hotels catering for winter sports. All have ski-rooms.

Fact boxes

Beneath each hotel description are the facts and figures which should help you to decide whether or not the hotel is in your price range and has the facilities that you require. Do confirm prices when you make your reservation.

Tel The first number is the area code used within Austria. When dialling from abroad, omit the initial 0 of this code.

Fax Most hotels now have a fax number which makes reservations swifter and easier.

Location The setting of the hotel is described briefly; car parking facilities follow.

Introduction

Meals Most hotels offer all meals, but we have included some bed-and-breakfasts, too.

Prices These show two prices – from the cheapest single room in low season to the most expensive double room in high season. Do ask proprietors about special reductions.

Rooms We summarize the number and style of bedrooms available. Our lists of facilities in bedrooms do not cover ornaments such as flowers or consumables such as toiletries.

Facilities We list public rooms as well as outdoor and sporting facilities which are either part of the hotel or close by; facilities in the vicinity of the hotel feature at the end of the main section under **Nearby**.

Credit cards We use the following abbreviations for credit cards:
AE   American Express,
DC   Diners Club,
MC   Master Card (Access/Eurocard),
V   Visa (Barclaycard/Bank Americard/Carte Bleue)

Proprietors Where managers are employed, we name them.

Glossary of terms
Several German terms are used in our hotel descriptions.
Alm mountain hut
Appartment large bedroom with extra sitting area
Bio organic natural food; sometimes bedrooms where only natural fibres and materials are used
Burg castle
Jagd, Jäger hunting, hunter
Kachelofen traditional ceramic-tiled stove
Kur 'cure'; like a health-farm
Schloss castle
See lake
Stammtisch table for regulars, locals
Strudel Austria's famous dessert, served at all times; sometimes savoury
Stube, Stüble, Stüberl wood-panelled room where food and drinks are served
Tafelspitz boiled beef; along with *Schnitzel*, a national dish.

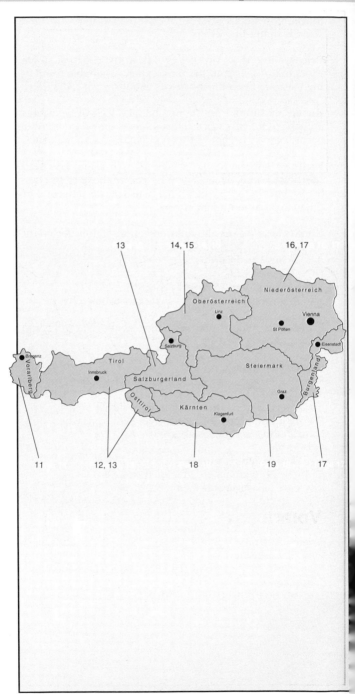

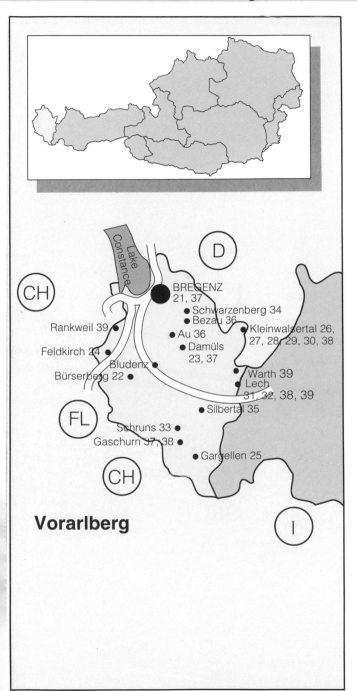

Vorarlberg

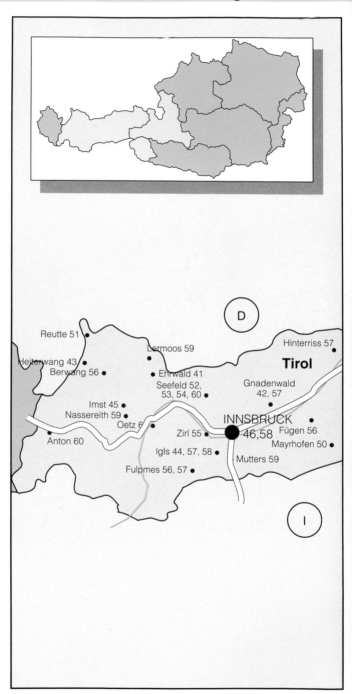

Mattsee 67 •   • Strasswalchen 83

D

Salzburgerland

• Ebbs 56

SALZBURG
69-75, 83

• Kufstein
48, 58

• Fuschl am See 81
• St Gilgen 76

Oberalm 83 •

Kitzbühel 58 •   • Leogang 82   Hallein 82 •

• Abtenau 81

Werfen 78 •   • Filzmoos 65

Wald 77, 84   Zell 79, 80, 84   Goldegg 66,82 •   • Altenmarkt 62

• Mittersill   Kaprun 82
68, 83   Dorfgastein 81 •   • Wagrain 84

• Kals 47
Matrei 59 •   Badgastein
63, 64, 81

O S T T I R O L

• Lienz 49

• Strassen 60

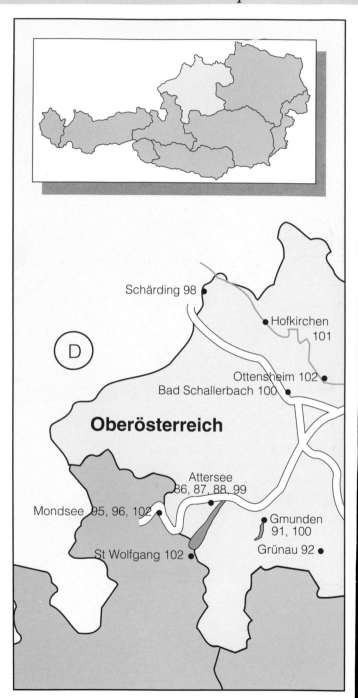

Schärding 98

Hofkirchen 101

D

Ottensheim 102

Bad Schallerbach 100

Oberösterreich

Attersee
86, 87, 88, 99

Mondsee 95, 96, 102

Gmunden
91, 100

Grünau 92

St Wolfgang 102

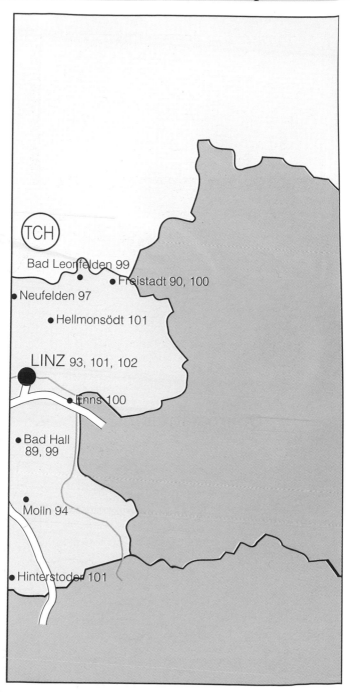

TCH

Bad Leonfelden 99

Freistadt 90, 100

Neufelden 97

Hellmonsödt 101

LINZ 93, 101, 102

Enns 100

Bad Hall
89, 99

Molln 94

Hinterstoder 101

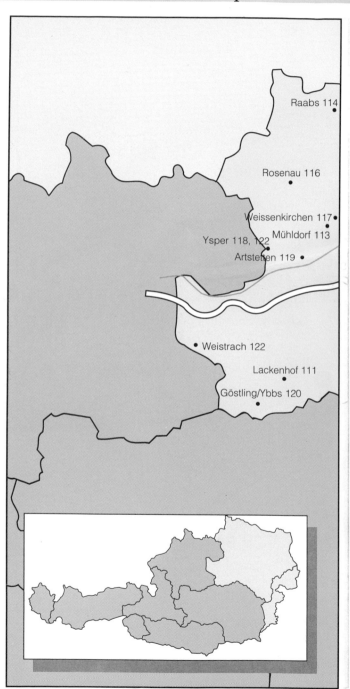

Raabs 114

Rosenau 116

Weissenkirchen 117

Mühldorf 113

Ysper 118, 122

Artstetten 119

Weistrach 122

Lackenhof 111

Göstling/Ybbs 120

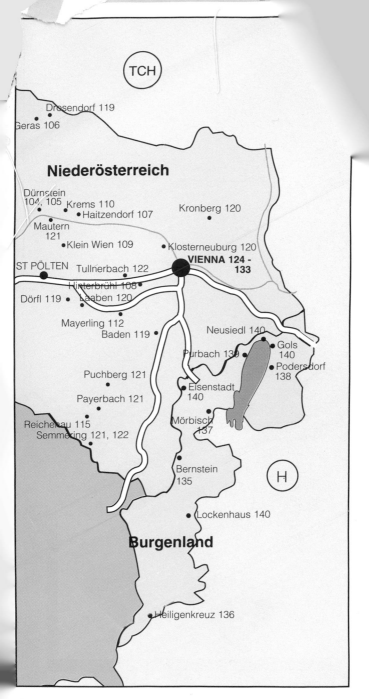

TCH

Drosendorf 119

Geras 106

Niederösterreich

Dürnstein
104, 105 Krems 110
• Haitzendorf 107

Kronberg 120
•

Mautern
121
• Klein Wien 109
• Klosterneuburg 120
**VIENNA 124 -
133**

ST PÖLTEN Tullnerbach 122

Hinterbrühl 108 •

Dörfl 119 • Laaben 120

Mayerling 112
Baden 119 •

Neusiedl 140
• Gols
140

Purbach 130 •
• Podersdorf
138

Puchberg 121

Eisenstadt
140

Payerbach 121

Mörbisch
137

Reichenau 115
Semmering 121, 122

Bernstein
135

H

• Lockenhaus 140

Burgenland

• Heiligenkreuz 136

17

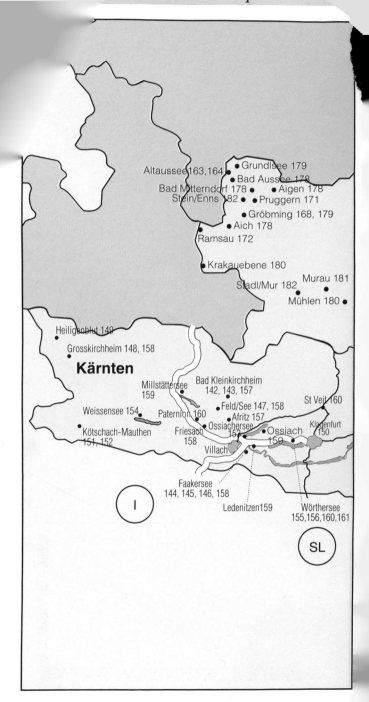

Altaussee 163, 164 ● ● Grundlsee 179
Bad Aussee 178
Bad Mitterndorf 178 ● ● Aigen 178
Stein/Enns 182 ● ● Pruggern 171
● Gröbming 168, 179
● Aich 178
Ramsau 172

● Krakauebene 180

Stadl/Mur 182 ● Murau 181

Mühlen 180 ●

● Heiligenblut 149

● Grosskirchheim 148, 158

Kärnten

Millstättersee 159 ● Bad Kleinkirchheim 142, 143, 157

St Veit 160

Weissensee 154 ● Paternion 160 ● Feld/See 147, 158

● Afritz 157

● Kötschach-Mauthen 151, 152 Friesach 158 ● Ossiachersee 159 ● Ossiach 159 Klagenfurt 150

Villach

Faakersee 144, 145, 146, 158

Ledenitzen 159

Wörthersee 155, 156, 160, 161

I

SL

18

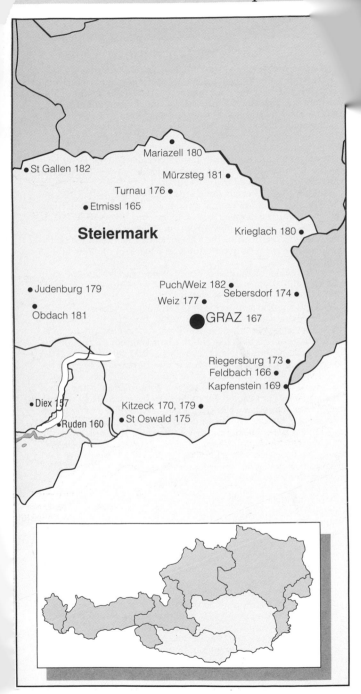

Mariazell 180

St Gallen 182

Mürzsteg 181

Turnau 176

Etmissl 165

Steiermark

Krieglach 180

Judenburg 179

Puch/Weiz 182

Sebersdorf 174

Weiz 177

Obdach 181

GRAZ 167

Riegersburg 173

Feldbach 166

Kapfenstein 169

Diex 157

Kitzeck 170, 179

St Oswald 175

Ruden 160

Vorarlberg

Hotels in Vorarlberg

The westernmost of Austria's Federal States, Vorarlberg is also (apart from Vienna) the smallest. What is more, it is virtually cut off from the rest of the country by the Arlberg mountains. Bordering on Germany, Switzerland and Liechtenstein it is an international playground with excellent tourist facilities.

One unique area is the Kleinwalsertal, which is itself cut off from Vorarlberg by more high mountains. The only road in is from Germany via Oberstdorf. Although politically part of Austria, this valley is economically part of Germany so all homes have both a German dialling code and postcode, as well as Austrian ones. Prices are quoted in Deutschmarks.

Among the numerous family-run establishments that did not quite qualify for a full entry for the guide is the Alpenhof Zimba in Brand which is popular with families and hikers (Tel (05559) 351, fax 35140, 23 rooms). Younger folk enjoy the lively atmosphere in the heart of the village at the Jägerheim which has plain rooms but a busy restaurant and bar (Tel (05559) 217, 13 rooms).

In the hamlet of Damüls is Zum Glöckle, tucked into the steep side of a hill, a short walk from the ski-lifts of this remote resort (Tel (05510) 380, fax 562, 8 rooms).

In Egg, a useful stopover is the Post, near the crossroads in the middle of the village (Tel (05512) 2230, fax 223012, 25 rooms). Lech am Arlberg is a fashionable resort, yet still has small family-run bed-and-breakfasts like the Pension Waldhof in Zug, owned by the head of the ski-school, Herr Schneider (Tel (05583) 2704, 11 rooms) or the Pension Helvetia where Herbert Tschugnall is a well-known summer walking guide (Tel (05583) 2666, 5 rooms). Another favourite, and handy for the *Tenniszentrum* is the Bickel family's Hotel Alexandra (Tel (05583) 2848, fax 3150, 19 rooms).

Schruns is another skier's paradise and Landhaus Pöschl enjoys regular repeat visits from downhillers who appreciate being in what is little more than a private house, a few steps from the Zamang-Hochjoch-Bahn (Tel (05556) 2807, 5 rooms). Bigger spenders head for the Alpenhof Messmer, an impressive and luxurious hotel above the town with splendid health spa and restaurant (Tel (05556) 2664, 39 rooms).

For further details about the area, contact:
Vorarlberg-Tourismus,
Römerstrasse 7/1,
A-6901 Bregenz
Tel (05574) 425250
Fax (05574) 425255

This page acts as an introduction to the features and hotels of Vorarlberg and gives brief recommendations of good hotels that for one reason or another have not made a full entry. The long entries for this state – covering the hotels we are most enthusiastic about – start on the next page. But do not neglect the shorter entries starting on page 36: these are all hotels that we would happily stay at.

Vorarlberg

Castle hotel, Bregenz

Deuring Schlössle

'Dramatic' was our reaction to this 17thC castle, up in the old part of Bregenz, overlooking Lake Constance. The scale is huge. The breakfast room looks like a medieval hall with a ceiling over 6 metres high, ancient beams, and walls over 1 metre thick. We expected to see m'lord and lady with their retinue instead of just tables and chairs beneath the swords, pikes and minstrel gallery. The bedrooms are more like suites, furnished with silk fabrics and antiques. Some are large enough for a dozen people to waltz in, others are cosier; each is special.

The food matches the surroundings. Ernst Huber was Austria's chef of the year back in 1984 when he cooked at the famous Zoll Restaurant in Bregenz. In 1989, along with his equally-talented son, Heino, he took over this castle. Like all top chefs, the Hubers use the best of local produce "but the Vorarlberg is not that rich in traditional dishes, so we invent our own or adapt ideas from chefs of the Austro-Hungarian emperors." The result is natural and light since they cut back on butter and cream. The dungeon-like wine cellar holds a valuable collection of international vintages.

Nearby old Upper Town; lake; Pfänder mountain.

6900 Bregenz, Ehre-Guta-Platz 4
Tel (05574) 47800
Fax (05574) 4780080
Location on medieval square in old town; car parking outside
Meals breakfast, lunch, dinner
Prices rooms AS1350-2700 with breakfast; meals from AS350
Rooms 13 suites; all have bath or shower, central heating, phone, TV

Facilities 2 dining-rooms, sitting-room, bar; terrace
Credit Cards AE, DC, MC, V
Children accepted
Disabled not suitable
Pets accepted; not in restaurant
Closed never
Languages English, French, Italian, Spanish
Proprietors Huber family

Vorarlberg

❊ **Mountain hotel, Bürserberg** ❊

Berghotel Schillerkopf

"Felt at home instantly" was the reaction of our inspector, who drove up the switchbacks to reach this hotel at the end of a long day. Not only was Christine Bosek happy to show off her domaine, even other guests were welcoming. One enthused about the garden, another about the indoor swimming-pool. It is the sort of place to settle into and relax, where attention to detail ranges from hand-carved ceiling panels to bright rugs on top of wall-to-wall carpets. All this and a terrific view over Bludenz some 6 km away.

The original *Gasthof* owned by Herr Bosek's parents burned down, so the present building dates from 1977, the annexe from 1983. Sporty types are kept happy with an all-weather tennis court plus horses; in winter, guests ski out and ski back, or spend the day in one of the other resorts around Bludenz. Special events range from barbecues to a *Bauernbüffet* (country buffet), from music in the basement bar to breakfast in a forest glade. Book one of the refurbished bedrooms, with a view over the valley or straight up the mountain. There is a large contingent of Dutch among the regulars of all ages.

Nearby winter sports, hiking, tennis, riding.

6700 Bürserberg
Tel (05552) 63104
Fax (05552) 67487
Location above Bürserberg, dizzy views over valley; car parking outside
Meals breakfast, lunch, dinner, snacks
Prices rooms AS410-1600 with breakfast; DB&B from AS510; reductions for children; meals from AS120
Rooms 18 suites, 8 double, 1 single; all have bath or shower, central heating, phone, radio; TV on request **Facilities** dining-room, sitting-room, bar, TV room, table-tennis room, terrace; garden, health and fitness areas, indoor swimming-pool **Credit Cards** not accepted **Children** very welcome **Disabled** not suitable **Pets** not accepted **Closed** Oct to mid-Dec; after Easter to mid-June **Languages** English, some French **Proprietors** Bosek family

Vorarlberg

❄ **Resort hotel, Damüls** ❄

Alpenhotel Mittagspitze

Access to Damüls has been easier since a new road was built in the mid-1980s. This is one of the highest resorts in Austria but the straggling village lacks a heart. Just below the church is this hotel, built in 1958 and named for the 2095-metre mountain straight across the ravine.

'Another dark, rather old-fashioned interior' was our inspector's first impression. That refers to the entrance. 'Strikingly modern, Italian influence' was her reaction to the restaurant and bar. Glasses glitter against a mirror, reflecting light on to the white walls. In one room, cushions and curtains are in patterns of deep purple, black and red; in another, wooden chairs are painted peacock-blue. Even the menu covers are fuchsia. Only the white stove looks typically Austrian.

Guests, mainly from Italy and France, include families who are now bringing their grandchildren. No doubt they approve of the changes, such as the hyacinth-blue fabrics and bleached wood in some bedrooms, the wicker chairs and pale pink and lilac colours in others. What remains the same is the 2-minute run down through the woods to the Uga ski lift.

Nearby Oberdamüls ski-lift, winter sports, hiking.

6884 Damüls
Tel (05510) 211
Fax (05510) 21120
Location on road in middle of Damüls; car parking outside, garage
Meals breakfast, lunch, dinner, snacks
Prices DB&B AS560–1600; reductions for children; meals from AS120
Rooms 20 double; all have bath or shower, central heating, phone, TV, radio
Facilities 2 dining-rooms, sitting-room, bar, terrace; sauna and solarium
Credit Cards AE, DC, MC, V
Children very welcome
Disabled not suitable
Pets accepted
Closed mid-Oct to early Dec; 4 weeks after Easter; restaurant only, Wed
Languages English, French, Italian
Proprietor Josef Madlener

Vorarlberg

Bed-and-breakfast hotel, Feldkirch

Alpenrose

This is just the sort of hotel we always hope to find in a pretty old town but seldom do. Located in the pedestrian zone, at the end of a tiny cobbled passageway, roses climb along the yellow front and between green shutters. The Alpenrose has been in the same family for generations and the current owner, Mrs. Gutwinski, is making improvements all the time. In 1989 she put in a lift/elevator; she also bought the next-door building and redecorated it in her own admirable taste.

Every room is different. In number 26, for example, yellow makes the room seem bright despite small windows while soft grey-blue gives it warmth. Number 20 has dainty ribbon-patterned wallpaper while number 23 has a tiny balcony. Bathrooms are on the small side but well thought-out, with large mirrors and adequate shelf space. Even the corridors are pleasant, with 19thC portraits and furniture.

Regulars include businessmen and -women and bookings must be made well in advance of the June Schubertiade festival, when many rooms are taken by artists, and you may even hear singers and musicians practising.

Nearby cathedral, Katzenturm, Rathaus, Schattenburg castle.

6800 Feldkirch, Rosengasse 6
Tel (05522) 22175
Fax (05522) 221755
Location in pedestrian area in old town; car parking outside or with hotel permit
Meals breakfast, snacks
Prices rooms AS550-1100 with breakfast
Rooms 19 double, 5 single; all have bath or shower, central heating, phone, TV
Facilities 2 breakfast rooms, sitting-room

Credit Cards AE, DC, MC, V
Children welcome
Disabled easy access to Room 23; lift/elevator
Pets accepted
Closed never
Languages English, French, some Italian
Proprietor Mrs. Rosi Gutwinski

Vorarlberg

❋ **Resort hotel, Gargellen** ❋

Alpenhotel Heimspitze

Set across the river from the village, the hotel has an atmosphere of seclusion, with a large garden and nothing but mountains behind. Originally a simple pension, it was rebuilt in 1969 in a traditional style but with modern spaciousness. The family like to collect: plenty of china, some pewter, and hundreds of ducks. That is Frau Thöny's hobby and she has examples from all over the world. There are even ducks in the sauna.

She has also chosen the furnishings for the bedrooms: oatmeal-coloured carpeting with woven rugs on top, a panel of fabric on a wall to match the curtains, and bed linen of pale pink, yellow, or blue. Even the single rooms are special, with painted furniture. And everyone finds flowers, chocolates or schnapps on arrival. There are two dining-rooms and a basement bar but the most popular room is the century-old, candle-lit *Maises-Stüble* with tiny wildflower pictures and inlaid-wood tables. The award-winning kitchen produces home-made jams, *Stollen* and a choice of 5 or 6 different cakes plus a menu that changes daily. In summer, children climb on the adventure playground and look for frogs in the nearby pond.
Nearby winter sports, hiking.

6787 Gargellen
Tel (05557) 6319
Fax (05557) 631920
Location across bridge, on east side of valley; car parking outside and covered
Meals breakfast, lunch, dinner, snacks
Prices DB&B from AS750-2500; reductions for children; meals from AS200
Rooms 2 suites, 15 double, 3 single; all have bath or shower, central heating, phone; some have hairdriers; TV on request
Facilities 2 dining-rooms, sitting-room, bar; playground, terrace, garden, health and massage area
Credit Cards AE, DC, MC
Children very welcome
Disabled not suitable
Pets not accepted
Closed mid-Oct to mid-Dec; mid-April to mid-June
Languages English, French, Italian
Proprietors Thöny family

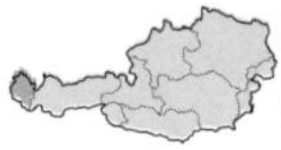

Vorarlberg

❄ **Traditional chalet, Kleinwalsertal** ❄

Sonnenberg

Every now and then we like a place so much we are tempted to keep it just for ourselves. This is it. Set high above the village of Hirschegg, the approach is up one of the steepest hills we have ever driven, or walked. When we arrived in summer, the garden was abloom with daisies, poppies, and iris. Kurt, from Germany, and Martine, from Alsace, take understandable delight in showing off their house, which dates back to 1530.

Ceilings are low and the ancient wood creaks with every step up to the bedrooms; each has a different colour scheme, but all have canopied four-poster beds plus bathrobes and walking sticks. Some hotel bedrooms are just for sleeping; these are comfortable enough to spend time in, though guests also relax in the basement sitting-room, where picture windows look straight across the valley. A small swimming-pool is like a grotto, built into a wall of rock.

Tables in the two snug dining-rooms are shared, so guests get to know one another over leisurely evening meals. Once a week there are gourmet suppers when the chef produces half-a-dozen courses of French, Italian or regional specialities.

Nearby winter sports, hiking.

6992 Hirschegg, Kleinwalsertal, Am Berg 26
Tel (05517) 5433
Fax (05517) 543333
Location on west side of valley above Hirschegg; car parking across street
Meals breakfast, dinner, snacks
Prices rooms DM88-260 with breakfast; DB&B DM150-220; reductions for children
Rooms 2 suites, 16 double, 1 single; all have bath or shower, central heating, phone, TV, hairdrier, radio
Facilities dining-room, sitting-room, conservatory; indoor swimming-pool; terrace, garden
Credit Cards not accepted
Children accepted
Disabled not suitable
Pets small dogs only
Closed Nov to mid-Dec; mid-Apr to mid-May
Languages English, French
Proprietors Krieger family

Vorarlberg

❋   **Resort hotel, Kleinwalsertal**   ❋

Steinbock

Hans Vogler believes in having "a good life as well as a good business." He is from Allgäu, just over the German border, his wife is from the Bregenzerwald, and they spent years working in Sweden and the Benelux countries before buying a small guesthouse here in 1981. Expansion and improvements have been made carefully; for example, the lower-level bar is so well-insulated that guests in the restaurant above cannot hear the music. Each bedroom comes with an umbrella and guests can use the washing-machine and tumble-drier in the basement. Furnishings throughout are solid and comfortable.

Breakfast is a feast. Cut your own slices of *Bio* (organic) breads and cheeses, scoop butter from its wooden tub and boil or fry an egg on the little table-stove. Cereals are stored in the drawers of an old cupboard, there are several bowls of dried and fresh fruits, and 6 types of tea. The Sunday barbecue is an institution; Herr Vogler presides, cooking *Bratwurst*, chicken and steaks while a band plays all the old favourites. Tall, with a handle-bar moustache, he enjoys playing 'mine host'. "My hobbies in winter are cross-country and downhill skiing . . . and throwing snowballs."
Nearby winter sports, hiking, tennis.

6993 Mittelberg, Kleinwalsertal, Bödmerstr 46
Tel (05517) 5033
Fax (05517) 3164
Location in southernmost village of valley; ample car parking
Meals breakfast, lunch, dinner, snacks
Prices rooms DM50-100 with breakfast; DB&B from DM90-125; reductions for children; meals from DM30
Rooms 22 double, all have bath or shower, central heating, phone, TV, minibar, radio, safe
Facilities 2 dining-rooms, sitting-room, bar/disco, terrace; sauna, washing machine
Credit Cards not accepted
Children very welcome
Disabled not suitable **Pets** accepted **Closed** Nov to mid-Dec; 2 weeks after Easter
Languages English, Swedish
Proprietors Vogler family

Vorarlberg

Almhof Rupp

Friedhelm Rupp has won acclaim and 2 *toques* from *Gault Millau* for his cuisine. As well as the superb à la carte menu, the half-board menu is impressive with dishes such as asparagus with smoked salmon strips, calves' liver with Madeira sauce, and rhubarb strudel. Each week a different gala menu is offered, with 6 or 7 courses of Italian, French, or Austrian dishes. The wine list is as international as the food.

Built 25 years ago, this is no architectural gem, set just off the main road with the car park in front. The back overlooks a roaring mountain stream and the Kanzelwandbahn lift. Rooms are being renovated; out go the dark colours, in come panels of natural linen, white paint on the wood, and a carpet of cream and blue, creating an altogether lighter look. These have bright, white, roomy bathrooms with double wash-basins. In the bar, bench seats surround the circular open fireplace and look right into the restaurant. This retains the old-fashioned rustic look, with brown wood and orange curtains. Facing south, it is flooded with natural light in summer and lit by candles on winter evenings. Herr Rupp enjoys leading hiking tours in the summer.
Nearby winter sports, hiking.

6991 Riezlern, Kleinwalsertal
Tel (05517) 5004
Fax (05517) 3273
Location in middle of village; car parking outside
Meals breakfast, dinner, snacks
Prices rooms DM90-200 with breakfast; DB&B from DM120; reductions for children; meals from DM35
Rooms 28 double, 1 single; all have bath or shower, central heating, phone, TV, radio

Facilities 2 dining-rooms, bar, TV room, 2 games rooms, terrace; sauna, beauty treatment, small indoor pool
Credit Cards not accepted
Children very welcome
Disabled not suitable
Pets accepted; not in dining-room
Closed Nov to mid-Dec; after Easter to mid-May
Languages English, some French, Italian
Proprietor Friedhelm Rupp

Vorarlberg

❄ **Old farmhouse, Kleinwalsertal** ❄

s'Breitachhus

In winter, this looks like an iced gingerbread house; in summer clematis, roses, and geraniums cover the front. Bought by Harald and Christine Riezler 20 years ago, the building dates back over 300 years and has the darkened wood to prove it. Step across the deep porch, bend your head through the tiny doorway and you are inside a private home. Like most, it is furnished with an eclectic mixture of old and new. Pictures of children are everywhere but pride of place is given to the blown-up wedding photograph of the Riezlers in traditional Kleinwalsertal dress, with Christine wearing the special crown and green apron of the Walser bride.

Bedrooms come in all shapes and sizes and are prettily, if simply, decorated. Two have four-poster beds; all have balconies and modern bathrooms. Harald's menu is good home-style cooking with a choice for vegetarians and at breakfast, jams and wholemeal rolls arc home-made. Guests get to know one another, talking in the little sitting-room with its warming oven and eating in the honey-coloured, wood-panelled dining-room. Smokers, however, are expected to go outside for a puff.

Nearby Parsenn ski-lift, winter sports, hiking.

6991 Riezlern, Kleinwalsertal
Tel (05517) 6266
Fax (05517) 6266107
Location on hillside above Riezlern; ample car parking
Meals breakfast, dinner, snacks
Prices rooms DM48-150 with breakfast; in winter, DB&B only from DM90; reductions for children
Rooms 9 double, 1 single; all have bath or shower, central heating, phone

Facilities dining-room, sitting-room, TV room, smoking area, terrace; whirl-pool in cellar
Credit Cards not accepted
Children very welcome
Disabled not suitable
Pets not accepted
Closed Nov to early Dec (snow); 2-4 weeks after Easter
Languages some English, French
Proprietors Riezler family

Vorarlberg

❋ **Old house, Kleinwalsertal** ❋

Walser Stuba

The village of Riezlern is named for this family, one of the original Walsers who left Switzerland some 600 years ago. The owners of the Breitachhus just up the hill are cousins. Not surprisingly, this is a traditional household. In the 'Walser Marriage Gallery', the family tree on the wall dates back to the 16thC. A glass case displays the wedding crown, handed down through seven generations, along with the bridal dress. Once a week the family even gives a talk and slide show explaining the customs and history of the Kleinwalsertal.

Furnishings are exactly what is expected of a traditional country inn: enormous baskets of dried flowers, decorative carved wood and bench seating. Yet it was built in 1985, so most rooms are larger than in an old building and there is a glassed-in terrace next to the dining-room. Local game features on the menu, but a vegetarian dish is also offered and older folk can ask for smaller portions. At the other end of the age range, colouring pencils are provided so tiny children can draw on their special menus. The resident 'babysitter' is Laura, a noisy, yellow and blue parrot who does acrobatic tricks on her swing and shows off constantly.

Nearby Parsenn ski-lift, winter sports, hiking.

6991 Riezlern, Kleinwalsertal
Tel (05517) 53460
Fax (05517) 534613
Location on hillside above village of Riezlern; car parking outside
Meals breakfast, lunch, dinner, snacks
Prices DB&B DM84-210 with breakfast; reductions for children; meals from DM30
Rooms 20 double, 4 single; all have bath or shower, central heating, phone, TV, hairdrier, radio, safe
Facilities 3 dining-rooms, sitting-room, bar, terrace; fitness and health area; baby-sitting
Credit Cards AE, DC, MC, V
Children very welcome
Disabled some access
Pets accepted
Closed Nov to mid-Dec; restaurant only, Tues
Languages English
Proprietors Riezler family

Vorarlberg

❆ **Resort hotel, Lech am Arlberg** ❆

Silencehotel Angela

Many hotels promise great comfort and a 'home from home' ambience; few achieve both. This one does. "If guests want to have breakfast at noon, they can have it," says Luise Walch who, with her husband, Elmar, transformed this old farmhouse. They kept the back door, cracked with age, and put it behind the reception desk, along with a trumpeting angel and a big bell. There are, however, none of the rustic bits and pieces which all too often create a contrived and cluttered look.

Rooms are named for the mountain in view and all have different fabrics, from tartans to florals. The 'small' ones are far from cramped, while the new suites are handsome, with bold patterns standing out against a white and cream background. The penthouse has a kitchen and a maid will come in to cook breakfast. Dinner in the pink and pine-green dining-room runs to 6 courses.

Just above the village, the hotel is surrounded by meadows full of gentian and cows. Herr Walch is a local and leads walking tours; as a former head of the ski school he can advise on the best places to ski, starting right from the door.

Nearby Schlegelkopf lift, winter sports, hiking.

6764 Lech am Arlberg, 62
Tel (05583) 2407
Fax (05583) 240715
Location up twisting road on hillside above town; ample car parking; indoor garage
Meals breakfast, lunch, dinner, snacks
Prices rooms AS620-1200 with breakfast; reductions for children; meals from AS100
Rooms 28 double, 2 single; all have bath or shower, central heating, phone, TV, minibar, radio, safe, scales
Facilities dining-room, sitting-room, bar, games-room, terrace; large health and fitness area
Credit Cards not accepted
Children very welcome
Disabled not suitable
Pets not accepted
Closed Oct, Nov; May, June
Languages English, French, Italian
Proprietors Walch family

Vorarlberg

❅ **New hotel, Lech-Zug** ❅

Hotel Rote Wand

Our inspector found no greater contrast between old and new anywhere else in Austria. Josef Walch Jr's restaurant is as traditional as you can get and famous for fondues. The hotel provides the 'shock of the new'. Colours are fresh turquoise and green, soft lilac and violet, set off by white walls and the palest of wood. Fabrics are checks and plaids. Even the basics are turned into features: stair railings are painted aquamarine while upright radiators look like organ pipes. Bedrooms are straight out of a design magazine with custom-made furniture and beds are upstairs in the split-level galleries.

The emphasis is on health and fitness. Photographs of Jane Fonda-types adorn the reception area and there is a wide choice of exercise programmes, from aerobics and jogging to water gymnastics and weight training. In winter, anyone opting out of skiing can practice golf shots in the basement driving range or play tennis on the nearby indoor courts. Children, too, are well-catered for. There is a large swimming-pool, an outdoor playground and a first-rate indoor playroom, with a resident nanny during the main holiday seasons.

Nearby winter sports, hiking, tennis.

6764 Lech-Zug am Arlberg
Tel (05583) 34350
Fax (05583) 343540
Location in hamlet of Zug, near Lech; car parking outside
Meals breakfast, lunch, dinner, snacks
Prices DB&B AS1550-2250; children under 6 free; meals from AS200
Rooms 34 double, all have bath and shower, central heating, phone, TV, minibar, hairdrier

Facilities 3 dining-rooms, sitting-room, bar, terrace; games-rooms, billiard table, indoor swimming-pool
Credit Cards DC
Children very welcome
Disabled very good access; lift/elevator **Pets** accepted
Closed Sept to early Dec; after Easter to 1 July **Languages** English, some French, some Italian **Proprietors** Josef Walch family

Vorarlberg

Hotel Krone

We have mixed feelings about the Krone. For convenience and history, this old tavern makes a good place to stay. There is no doubt that Robert Mayer is an above-average chef with one of the finest restaurants in the Montafon valley. As well as the traditional *Tafelspitz* (boiled beef), Mayer nods towards France when he delicately sauces *ris-de-veau* and poaches salmon and zander in garlic and tomato butter.

The *Montafonstube*, with its caramel-coloured, heavily-knotted pine panelling is a 'must' for visitors. The windows are leaded and the octagonal tables are inlaid with slate, which was used both as a stand for hot pans and as a chalk-board for farmers doing business on market-day. Upstairs, the ceiling of the *Krone-stube* is painted with signs of the zodiac.

By comparison, the bedrooms are straightforward, even boring. It takes more than parquet floors and Biedermeier beds to give character; perhaps some pictures on the virtually bare walls, a change of curtains, and some improvements to the bathrooms. The terrace garden is a plus, as is the location – just a few steps from the middle of the lovely old part of Schruns.

Nearby old town; Montafon ski area, winter sports, hiking.

6780 Schruns
Tel (05556) 2255
Fax (05556) 4879
Location near middle of town, next to river; car parking across the street
Meals breakfast, lunch, dinner, snacks
Prices rooms AS400-850 with breakfast; DB&B from AS540; reductions for children; meals from AS200
Rooms 8 double, 1 single; all have bath or shower, central heating, phone, minibar, radio; TV on request
Facilities 2 dining-rooms, sitting-room, terrace
Credit Cards DC, MC
Children welcome but not suitable
Disabled not suitable
Pets accepted
Closed mid-Oct to mid-Dec; after Easter to early June
Languages English, French, some Italian
Proprietors Mayer family

Vorarlberg

❄   **Old inn, Schwarzenberg**   ❄

Gasthof Hirschen

You can't miss this 18thC inn, opposite the church on the main crossroads in the village. The whole of Schwarzenberg is a national treasure, with its wooden-shingled houses so typical of the Bregenzerwald valley. Few hotels succeed in being all things to all people but the Fetz family, who have been here for 100 years, manage to do just that. Locals pop in for a drink in the low-ceilinged *Jägerstube* but for special occasions book into the restaurant, rated one of the best in the area.

Families arrive in winter for ski holidays but during the summer the hotel is filled with couples. There is even a choice of style: traditional in the old house, where bedrooms have antique beds and brass fittings; boldly modern in the annexe, where rooms are larger, perhaps with a skylight or a wrought-iron bed. Furnishings are in delicate shades of purple, blue, and green, with touches of bright pink or red. This is also where small business seminars are held, away from other guests.

Behind the village, the Hochälpelekopf is covered with ski runs; cross-country trails loop round the valley.

Nearby Angelika Kaufmann paintings, altar-piece in Baroque church; local museum.

6867 Schwarzenberg
Tel (05512) 29440
Fax (05512) 294420
Location in middle of charming, old village; car parking right outside
Meals breakfast, lunch, dinner, snacks
Prices rooms AS550-1500 with breakfast; DB&B AS830 in winter; reductions for children; meals from AS350
Rooms 13 double, 10 single, 5 suites; all have bath or shower, central heating, phone, TV, minibar, hairdrier, radio
Facilities 3 dining-rooms, sitting-room, *Stube*, terrace; sauna; seminar rooms
Credit Cards AE, DC, MC, V
Children very welcome
Disabled not suitable
Pets accepted
Closed mid-Nov to mid-Dec; restaurant only, Wed
Languages English, French, Italian
Proprietors Fetz family

Vorarlberg

❄ **Mountain lodge, Silbertal** ❄

Gasthof Kristberg

When everyone else has gone down to the valley and the cable car has stopped for the night, guests at this simple inn have the mountain to themselves. There are few other buildings on this slope high above Silbertal and just 100 m from the top of the Kristbergbahn. It is a family business: Herr Zudrell is host and his wife is in charge of the kitchen. Everything from eggs to meat comes from local farms. At the entrance, a display case overflows with their children's ski trophies. The atmosphere is more 'home' than 'hotel'. Bedrooms in the new wing are cheerful, with a teddy-bear pattern on children's duvets; the few old rooms with shared bath and lavatory facilities are ideal for groups of friends or families who appreciate a bargain.

"You have to want to be with other people," Silvi, one of the daughters, told us in her excellent English. Guests spend time talking after dinner, there are games for children, and sometimes a torch-lit evening walk in winter. In summer, farmers in green boots congregate at the *Stammtisch* and walkers stop for cold drinks. Informality is the rule; this is not for anyone wearing designer clothes and expecting five-star service.

Nearby winter sports, hiking trails, Kristbergbahn.

6780 Silbertal, Kristberg 240
Tel (05556) 722900
Fax (05556) 722905
Location on mountain-side above Silbertal valley; phone ahead for access by car, otherwise 5 minutes' walk from cable car
Meals breakfast, lunch, dinner, snacks
Prices rooms AS240-1400 with breakfast; DB&B from AS345-840; reductions for children; meals from AS115

Rooms 12 double, 3 single, 1 separate cabin; all have central heating, phone; most have bath or shower; TV on request
Facilities dining-room, sitting-room, bar, TV room, terrace; small gymnasium **Credit Cards** not accepted **Children** very welcome **Disabled** not suitable **Pets** accepted **Closed** Nov to mid-Dec; 1 week after Easter; 2 weeks May
Languages English, French
Proprietors Zudrell family

Vorarlberg

Haus Alpina

More like a home than a hotel. Some bedrooms have traditional painted furniture, others are modern, but all have up-to-date bathrooms. Fitness area in the basement and cross-country skiing from the door through surrounding meadows.

■ 6883 Au, Rehmen 30 **Tel** (05515) 2365 **Fax** (05515) 236571 **Meals** breakfast **Prices** rooms AS260-700 with breakfast **Rooms** 16, all with shower, central heating, phone **Credit cards** not accepted **Closed** Nov to mid-Dec **Languages** French

---

Gasthof Sonne

On the edge of a pretty Bregenzerwald village, this clever blend of old and new has painted shutters and windowboxes of red geraniums facing the road. Behind is an extension with games rooms plus health and fitness spa. Good cross-country skiing.

■ 6870 Bezau **Tel** (05514) 2262 or 2470 **Fax** (05514) 2912 **Meals** breakfast, lunch, dinner, snacks **Prices** rooms AS445-800 with breakfast; meals from AS125 **Rooms** 30, all with bath or shower, central heating, phone, TV, radio **Credit cards** not accepted **Closed** Nov **Languages** English

---

Gasthof Rössle

The Bargehr family have given a facelift to this inn, located next to the church. Fresh paint outside and new but rustic-style bedrooms inside. A good base for Klostertal skiers and the imaginative menus are also attracting attention.

■ 6751 Braz bei Bludenz, Arlbergstr 67 **Tel** (05552) 8105 **Fax** (05552) 8470 **Meals** breakfast, lunch, dinner, snacks **Prices** rooms AS360-800 with breakfast; meals from AS110 **Rooms** 10, all with bath or shower, central heating, phone; TV by request **Credit cards** not accepted **Closed** Oct; restaurant only, Mon, Tues **Languages** English

---

Gasthof Traube Braz

In winter, skiers head for the Sonnenkopf in the Klostertal; families hand over small children to the permanent nanny; but everyone enjoys the ambitious mixture of regional and new-Austrian cooking. Plain bedrooms, attractive public rooms.

■ 6751 Braz bei Bludenz, Klostertalerstr **Tel** (05552) 8103 **Fax** (05552) 810340 **Meals** breakfast, lunch, dinner, snacks **Prices** rooms AS480-1560 with breakfast; meals from AS110 **Rooms** 26, with bath or shower, central heating, phone, radio **Credit cards** not accepted **Closed** Nov **Languages** English, French, Italian, Spanish

Vorarlberg

Mountain hotel, Eichenberg bei Bregenz

Hotel Schönblick

Worth staying for the breathtaking views across Lake Constance. The terrace of this 13-year-old hotel attracts tourists and locals alike but the Hehle family also have a fine restaurant, adequate bedrooms and an indoor swimming-pool.

■ 6911 Eichenberg bei Bregenz **Tel** (05574) 45965 **Fax** (05574) 459657 **Meals** breakfast, lunch, dinner, snacks **Prices** rooms AS430-1100 with breakfast; meals from AS130 **Rooms** 22, all with bath or shower, central heating, phone, TV; some with minibar **Credit cards** not accepted **Closed** Jan; restaurant only, Mon **Languages** English, French

---

❄ Chalet hotel, Damüls ❄

Berghotel Madlener

High in the Bregenzerwald and just out of the village, this is a first-rate example of a new hotel built in the familiar chalet style. Ceilings and walls are panelled in pale wood, logs blaze in corner fireplaces, bedrooms are bright with flowery fabrics.

■ 6884 Damüls, Haus 22 **Tel** (05510) 2210 **Fax** (05510) 22115 **Meals** breakfast, lunch, dinner, snacks **Prices** rooms AS420-950 with breakfast; meals from AS120 **Rooms** 26, all with bath or shower, central heating, phone; TV on request **Credit cards** not accepted **Closed** Nov **Languages** English

---

❄ Mountain resort hotel, Gaschurn ❄

Landhotel Älpili

There are two Älpilis on the edge of town, the old barn-turned-restaurant and the new luxury hotel next door. Furnishings are striking: pale pink, green and white for the bedrooms (all large), and bold green and purple for the dining room.

■ 6793 Gaschurn **Tel** (05558) 87330 **Fax** (05558) 873371 **Meals** breakfast, lunch, dinner, snacks **Prices** rooms AS450-2700 with breakfast; meals from AS150 **Rooms** 22, all with bath and shower, central heating, phone, TV, minibar **Credit cards** not accepted **Closed** mid-Oct to mid-Dec; after Easter to mid-May **Languages** English

---

❄ Resort village hotel, Gaschurn ❄

Hotel Monika

Monika Bergauer refurbished her hotel 8 years ago, keeping the golden pine panelling but adding soft blue fabrics to the dining room. Bedrooms remain cramped. Indoor health spa, outdoor swimming-pool; 100m from Silvretta Nova gondola.

■ 6793 Gaschurn **Tel** (05558) 8291 **Fax** (05558) 8126 **Meals** breakfast, lunch, dinner, snacks **Prices** rooms AS340-2000 with breakfast; meals from AS120 **Rooms** 24, all with bath or shower, central heating, phone, TV **Credit cards** AE, DC, MC, V **Closed** never **Languages** English

Vorarlberg

❄   Mountain resort hotel, Gaschurn   ❄

Hotel Saladina

Only a minute's walk from the Versettla gondola station, this has a gloomy outside but a cheery interior, lightened by large windows and honey-coloured pine. With only 9 suites, the sauna, whirlpool and outdoor pool are never crowded.
■ 6793 Gaschurn **Tel** (05558) 8204 **Fax** (05558) 820421 **Meals** breakfast, lunch, dinner, snacks **Prices** rooms AS320-1200 with breakfast; meals from AS145 **Rooms** 9 suites, all with bath or shower, central heating, phone, TV, minibar, radio **Credit cards** not accepted **Closed** Nov to mid-Dec **Languages** English

---

❄   Town hotel, Kleinwalsertal   ❄

Hotel Jagdhof

A central meeting place, across from the casino. The café, restaurants and terrace here are always busy. Bedrooms, however, are quiet, with balconies and plenty of storage space. Fine health and fitness spa, but expansion is planned.
■ 6991 Riezlern, Walserstr 27 **Tel** (05517) 5603 **Fax** (05517) 3348 (code from Germany 08329) **Meals** breakfast, lunch, dinner, snacks **Prices** rooms DM80-220 with breakfast; meals from DM15 **Rooms** 25, all with bath or shower, central heating, phone, TV **Credit cards** not accepted **Closed** 15 Nov to 15 Dec **Languages** some English, some French

---

❄   Mountain resort hotel, Lech am Arlberg   ❄

Brunnenhof

Master chef Balthasar Thaler and Heinz Auer make the finest cooking partnership in Voralberg; Angelika Thaler runs this fashionable hotel. Pale carved wood, dried flowers, and subtle fabrics are artfully combined. Expensive.
■ 6764 Lech am Arlberg **Tel** (05583) 2349 **Fax** (05583) 234959 **Meals** breakfast, lunch, dinner, snacks **Prices** rooms AS1000-3500 with breakfast; meals from AS450 **Rooms** 21, all with bath or shower, central heating, phone, TV, radio, safe **Credit cards** AE, DC **Closed** June to Nov **Languages** English, some French

---

❄   Resort hotel, Lech am Arlberg   ❄

Hotel Haldenhof

Daily European newspapers and international dishes on the menu reflect the regular clientele. Heavy brown timbers, autumnal colours and thick rugs on quarry tile floors create a warmth matched by the Schwärzlers' welcome. Near ski school.
■ 6764 Lech am Arlberg **Tel** (05583) 24440 **Fax** (05583) 244421 **Meals** breakfast, lunch, dinner, snacks **Prices** rooms AS350-860 **Rooms** 22, all with bath or shower, central heating, phone, TV, radio **Credit cards** not accepted **Closed** after Easter to early July; mid-Sept to late Nov **Languages** English, French, Italian

Vorarlberg

❋   Mountain resort hotel, Lech am Arlberg   ❋

Hotel Madlochblick

Understandably popular thanks to steady upgrading of facilities. There are cheerful sitting areas with lots of wood, deep chairs and open fireplaces. Bedrooms are decorated in neutral beige. More suited to adults than families. Good new fitness area.

■ 6764 Lech am Arlberg **Tel** (05583) 2220 **Fax** (05583) 3416 **Meals** breakfast, lunch, dinner, snacks **Prices** rooms AS350-2500, with breakfast **Rooms** 25, all with bath, central heating, phone, TV, hairdrier, radio, safe **Credit cards** not accepted **Closed** 20 Sept to early Dec; end April to early July **Languages** English

---

Restaurant with rooms, Rankweil

Gasthof Mohren

Roland Hofer's cooking is the attraction here. Menus include both traditional Voralberg specialties and lighter dishes. Modern, practical and comfortable rooms. A good base for touring and for Bregenz and Feldkirch music festivals.

■ 6830 Rankweil, Stiegstr 17 **Tel** (05522) 44275 **Fax** (05522) 442755 **Meals** breakfast, lunch, dinner, snacks **Prices** rooms AS450-1500 with breakfast; meals from AS180 **Rooms** 15, all with bath or shower, central heating, phone, TV, radio **Credit cards** DC, MC, V **Closed** restaurant only, Mon **Languages** English

---

❋   Chalet hotel, Warth am Arlberg   ❋

Hotel Lechtaler Hof

The Brenner's hotel may be small, but the rooms are certainly comfortable, with deep balconies to soak up the sun. The accent is on sport, with special week-long adventure holidays for horse-lovers, walkers, mountain bikers. Ski-school next to the hotel.

■ 6767 Warth am Arlberg **Tel** (05583) 2677 **Fax** (05583) 36868 **Meals** breakfast, lunch, dinner, snacks **Prices** rooms AS350-1820 with breakfast **Rooms** 15, all with bath or shower, central heating, TV, radio, minibar **Credit cards** not accepted **Closed** Oct to early Dec; after Easter to early May **Languages** English, French

---

❋   Mountain resort hotel, Warth am Arlberg   ❋

s'Walserberg Hotel

Warth is a remote village high in the mountains, so the Walch family provide a lot for guests, from a café and pizzeria to a bakery and hairdresser. Ski from the door in winter; learn to paint in summer. Simple comforts, good for families.

■ 6767 Warth am Arlberg **Tel** (05583) 35020 **Fax** (05583) 350222 **Meals** breakfast, lunch, dinner, snacks **Prices** rooms AS380-1750 with breakfast; meals from AS120 **Rooms** 29, all with bath or shower, central heating, phone, TV **Credit cards** not accepted **Closed** Nov to mid-Dec; after Easter to June **Languages** English

Tirol

Hotels in the Tyrol

The Tyrol (*Tirol* in German) must be Austria's most famous region around the world, thanks to spectacular scenery, excellent skiing and photogenic villages.

The simple places can still offer sound value for money as we found in Imst, where SOS, the world famous children's charity, set up its first village for orphans. Near the main gate is Die Hohe Warte (Tel (05412) 2414, 11 rooms) high on the Weinberg, with its own garden and a dedicated family running it.

Simplicity can also be an excuse for marking time. The Krone in Umhausen (Tel (05255) 5274, 6 rooms) is well known for its 17thC *Erkerzimmer*, complete with bow window and leaded glass. The bedrooms are bleak by contrast but the new generation of owners insists that they will upgrade them to the level that the rest of the house deserves. Also undergoing much-needed improvements is the Grünwalderhof (Tel (0512) 77304, fax 78078, 17 rooms) on the edge of Patsch, a small ski-resort near Innsbruck. The Wanner family, who are leasing the former hunting-lodge from the Graf Thurn und Taxis, have plenty of work to do.

Ehrwald is a fine, unspoiled resort at the foot of the Zugspitze, near the German border. Completely renovated, the chalet-style Stern has lots of well-carved new wood in the old style inside and overlooks the village green (Tel (05673) 2287, 30 rooms). Nearby, the Sporthotel Alpenhof shows the more modern face of Austrian tourism with its indoor pool, glass conservatories and family-oriented sporty atmosphere. (Tel (05673) 2747, fax 274752, 48 rooms).

Just as sporting, with the bonus of the Achensee lake right outside the door, is the Sporthotel Achenseehof (Tel (05246) 6209, fax 634835, 32 rooms) which can be reached first on the romantic 90-year old train from Jenbach, then by boat.

East Tyrol is a fragment of the Federal State that was cut off when South Tyrol was ceded to Italy in 1919. Lienz is the focal point at the meeting of the Isel and Drau Rivers. Solidly respectable is the 400-year old Romantik Hotel Traube (Tel (04852) 64444, fax 64184, 51 rooms) in the heart of the old town which makes a central base for exploring the area.

For further details of the area, contact:
Tirol Werbung,
Bozner Platz 6,
A-6010 Innsbruck.
Tel (0512) 5320.
Fax (0512) 5320150.

This page acts as an introduction to the features and hotels of Tyrol and gives brief recommendations of good hotels that for one reason or another have not made a full entry. The long entries for this state – covering the hotels we are most enthusiastic about – start on the next page. But do not neglect the shorter entries starting on page 56; these are all hotels that we would happily stay at.

Tirol

❊   **Old chalet hotel, Ehrwald**   ❊

Hotel Spielmann

Staying here is like staying with Austrian friends. The hotel is an old Tyrolean house, run as a hotel by a family that dates back to the 1600s. Spielmann father and son are a rare combination: both are well-known mountain climbers as well as first-class chefs. Set on the edge of the village and away from traffic, the traditionally-painted house is surrounded by meadows. Some rooms have dark wood, others have pale, but all, even the singles, have a balcony. Colour is added by fresh and dried flowers, straw dolls and the family collection of 19thC Tyrolean prints.

The restaurant has a sound reputation and features recipes from grandma's cookbook; ingredients such as herbs, lamb and home-smoked *Speck* come from their own farm. Home-made breads and jams await breakfasters and once a week, out come zither and guitar, "not because we have to but because *Stubenmusik* was played here long before tourism began." Children love the spotlessly-clean barns, playground and swimming-pool; parents are thankful for the washing-machine. Best of all is hiking with the Spielmanns, perhaps to spot game, eagles and wildflowers; or, in winter, climbing fresh snow on seal-skins.

Nearby Sonnenhang ski-lifts, ski-school; cross-country trails.

6632 Ehrwald
Tel (05673) 2225
Fax (05673) 290257
Location in meadows outside village; ample car parking
Meals breakfast, lunch, dinner, snacks
Prices rooms AS380-1200 with breakfast; DB&B from AS500-700; reductions for children; meals from AS180
Rooms 26 double, 4 single; all have bath or shower, central heating, phone, radio; TV on request
Facilities 2 dining-rooms, sitting-room, bar, 2 TV rooms, games-room, terrace, garden, sauna, heated outdoor swimming-pool
Credit Cards AE, DC, MC, V
Children very welcome
Disabled not suitable
Pets accepted
Closed Nov to mid-Dec; after Easter to late May
Languages English
Proprietors Spielmann family

Tirol

❄ **Country inn, Gnadenwald** ❄

Gasthof Michaelerhof

Even from the road we reckoned this would make a good place to stay and closer inspection proved us right. The Schiestls took over this farmhouse in 1965, turning it first into a restaurant, then a hotel. Louis Schiestl worked as a chef all over the world, in Istanbul and Nairobi, Japan and Sweden before settling in this tiny hamlet and marrying a local woman. Proof of his confidence is his 'open kitchen', visible through windows in the bar and the doorway opposite reception. Menus reflect his international career, with *Nasi goreng* from Indonesia, curry from India and smoked fish from Scandinavia alongside the familiar *Schnitzel* and *Tafelspitz*.

Similarly, animal skins from Africa lend an exotic touch to the traditional Austrian interior. Instead of one main restaurant, there are four little *Stuben*: one has a collection of wooden bowls, another French windows that open to the patio in summer. Only 10 minutes' drive from the middle of Innsbruck, this is as popular for Sunday lunch as it is for business visitors during the week. Bedrooms are comfortable if unexceptional. There are tennis courts, a playground and trails in the forest.

Nearby winter sports, hiking, mountaineering, riding.

6060 Gnadenwald
Tel (05223) 48128
Fax (05223) 481284
Location on plateau near Innsbruck; car parking outside
Meals breakfast, lunch, dinner, snacks
Prices rooms AS400-800 with breakfast; reductions for children; meals from AS150
Rooms 10 double, 2 single; all have bath or shower, central heating, phone; TV on request
Facilities 4 dining-rooms, sitting-room with TV, bar, terrace, tennis-courts
Credit Cards AE, DC
Children very welcome
Disabled not suitable
Pets accepted
Closed Nov to mid-Dec; 2 weeks after Easter
Languages English, some French, Italian
Proprietors Schiestl family

Tirol

❋ **Lakeside hotel, Heiterwang** ❋

Fischer Am See

Our hearts sank when we saw a camping and caravan site near this inn. Fortunately, it proved to be less intrusive than we feared. Apparently, some children like to sleep in a tent while their parents take bedrooms in the hotel. These are above-average in size, with comfortable beds and small but adequate bathrooms. Downstairs, a jolly line of red, black and white-striped socks hangs over the reception area. Like the bedrooms, the dining rooms are practical rather than pretty, though on our visit, vases of wildflowers brightened each table and an old rowing boat served as an unusual buffet-table for breakfast in the mornings and for salads in the evening. Views of trees, mountains and water fill the picture windows.

Below the terrace is a landing stage for launches that shuttle up and down the interconnecting lakes of Heiterwangsee and Plansee. No petrol engines are allowed, so fishing, canoeing and rowing are unspoilt; but at this altitude (1,000 m) the water is warm enough for swimming only in July and August. In winter, moon-lit cross-country skiing excursions on the lake finish with steaming *Glühwein* at the bar.

Nearby lake, fishing, rowing, hiking, wintersports.

6611 Heiterwang
Tel (05674) 5116
Location at end of lane, facing lake; ample car parking
Meals breakfast, lunch, dinner, snacks
Prices rooms AS400-800 with breakfast; DB&B from AS600; reductions for children; meals from AS165
Rooms 8 double, 3 single; all have bath or shower, central heating
Facilities 3 dining-rooms, sitting-room, bar, sauna, solarium
Credit Cards not accepted
Children very welcome
Disabled not suitable
Pets accepted
Closed mid-Oct to mid-Dec; last 2 weeks Jan
Languages English, some French, Italian
Proprietors Bunte family

Tirol

Schlosshotel Igls

"The best from Italy and England, Spain and Austria," is how Frau Beck describes the furnishings of this hotel. In less skilled hands that Euro-combination could spell disaster; luckily she has the innate talent of a top interior designer. Every corner of this hundred-year-old villa is used and architectural oddities become features: number 36, for example, has a little pine-panelled sitting room in the octagonal turret. Returning guests request favourite rooms: perhaps number 35 where the soft brown and white trellis pattern gives a masculine feel, or number 17, with huge semi-circular windows.

There is a place for every mood. The blue and gold drawing room is formal with high ceilings and antiques; the bar has an open fire and leather armchairs. Downstairs, the restaurant reminded our inspector of a ship's dining room, with curving walls and dark wood panelling. The swimming-pool is equally luxurious and, at the push of a button, a wall of glass disappears into the ground so swimmers can walk out into the garden. Close enough to Innsbruck for businessmen, there are golf courses and ski areas nearby. 'Outstanding' was the final verdict.

Nearby skiing, wintersports, golf, tennis.

6080 Igls
Tel (0512) 377217
Fax (0512) 378679
Location on edge of village in own park; car parking outside, some under cover
Meals breakfast, lunch, dinner, snacks
Prices DB&B AS1820-4600, reductions for children; meals from AS220
Rooms 19 double; all have bath and shower, central heating, phone, TV, radio, minibar, hairdrier
Facilities 2 dining-rooms, sitting-room, bar, terrace; large gymnasium, indoor swimming-pool
Credit Cards AE, DC, MC, V
Children welcome
Disabled easy access
Pets accepted
Closed Nov to mid-Dec; 4 weeks after Easter
Languages English, French, Italian
Proprietors Beck family

Tirol

❄ **Coaching inn, Imst** ❄

Hotel Post

Christa Pfeifer is the driving force behind the success of what was once Sprengenstein Castle. The old building, with its red and white chevrons on the shutters, seems steeped in history. Reception is at the top of the stairs, where the long, white corridor has a decorated ceiling and a gilded, wrought-iron gate. Antique chests of drawers, tables with huge vases of flowers, armchairs and mirrors create an ambience that is grand without being imposing.

Photographs do not do justice to the main dining room. Not only are the wood panels dense with hand-carved trees and leaves, there is also a collection of the hideous masks for which the town is famous. The *Schemenlauf* (parade of spirits) takes place at Shrovetide every 3 to 5 years right outside the hotel. Every summer, however, guests sit out on the extraordinary covered terrace, decked with vines and flowers.

Bedrooms are handsome, with highly-polished wood and plush Edwardian-style fabrics; bathrooms, however, are right up-to-date. A large garden and enormous indoor swimming-pool are an added bonus.

Nearby skiing, winter sports, hiking, tennis, squash, rafting, mountaineering, fishing; SOS Children's Village.

6460 Imst
Tel (05412) 2554
Fax (05412) 251955
Location in heart of village in own park; ample car parking
Meals breakfast, lunch, dinner, snacks
Prices rooms AS350-1200 with breakfast; DB&B from AS500; reductions for children; meals from AS180
Rooms 10 suites, 13 double, 3 single; all have bath or shower, central heating, phone; TV, minibar in large rooms
Facilities 2 dining-rooms, sitting-room, conference room, terrace; garden, indoor swimming-pool
Credit Cards AE, DC, MC, V
Children very welcome
Disabled not suitable
Pets accepted
Closed Nov to 1 Feb (approx)
Languages English, French, Italian
Proprietors Pfeifer family

Tirol

Weisses Rössl

Popular tourist spots are all too often short of hotels that are right for this guide. This one is all but perfect. Find it right in the middle of the medieval old town. Climb the wide, tiled staircase to the restaurant one floor up and you will meet Werner Plank, wrapped in a long white apron, moving among the happy eaters, his voice booming above their conversations.

Originally owned by his grandfather, hard times forced his father to sell this 600 year-old inn. Young Werner worked his way around the world, saving up to re-install the Planks at the sign of the White Horse. In 1983, he succeeded. The first step was to renovate the medieval building by rewiring, replumbing and exposing the 16thC beams. In 1992, the interior was completely repainted. Now the comfortable bedrooms have high ceilings, plain walls and soft blue curtains at the large windows. The restaurant is a meeting place for locals, who pop in for a chat and a game of cards. "They never look at the menu, just order the special of the day," whether it is home-made pasta, potato pancakes, or strudel. Breakfast in the old *Stube,* hung with Tyrolean paintings, or on the quiet terrace.

Nearby Goldenes Dachl, Olympic Museum, cathedral, Hofburg.

6020 Innsbruck, Kiebachgasse 8 in der Altstadt
Tel (0512) 583057
Fax (0512) 5830575
Location in heart of old town, semi-pedestrian zone; public car parking nearby
Meals breakfast, lunch, dinner, snacks
Prices rooms AS750-1400 with breakfast; reductions for children; meals from AS120
Rooms 14 double; all have bath or shower, central heating, phone, radio; TV on request
Facilities 2 dining-rooms, terrace
Credit Cards AE, MC, V
Children welcome
Disabled reasonable access; lift/elevator
Pets accepted
Closed 2 weeks Nov; 2 weeks after Easter
Languages English
Proprietors Plank family

Tirol

❋ **Mountain hotel, Kals** ❋

Gasthof Taurerwirt

Hoteliers have a theory that the secret of success is 'location, location, location'. This hotel in East Tyrol proves the point. The approach road is twisting and steep, past gushing waterfalls, isolated chapels and the meadow where 'Heidi' was filmed. Finally, it reaches this chalet-style building set at the head of a valley on the southern slopes of the Grossglockner. In summer, the silence is broken only by rushing streams and squeaking swallows.

Its popularity is not due to stylish furnishings. Bedrooms and public rooms could do with an update, though perhaps the outdoor types who stay here prefer the old-fashioned look. Certainly, they like to hike in the mountains, fish the rivers, and ski both downhill and cross-country. The enthusiasm of the Rogls is impressive. On bright summer mornings, a farmer's wife bakes bread at a nearby cabin for an outdoor breakfast. Children have a real adventure playground in the pine trees. The restaurant serves up hearty portions and, with the old family farm next door, the chef is never short of ingredients. A simple, no-nonsense base for a get-away-from-it-all holiday.

Nearby Glocknerblick lift, hiking, fishing, tennis.

9981 Kals am Grossglockner
Tel (04876) 226
Fax (04876) 22611
Location the last hotel at head of valley, surrounded by meadows; ample car parking
Meals breakfast, lunch, dinner, snacks
Prices DB&B AS320-1280; reductions for children; meals from AS120
Rooms 20 double; all have bath or shower, phone; 10 double in annexe have communal facilities
Facilities dining-room, 2 sitting-rooms, bar, TV room, terrace; garden; sauna, table-tennis room, play-room, tennis courts
Credit Cards MC
Children very welcome
Disabled not suitable
Pets accepted
Closed mid-Oct to mid-Dec; after Easter to mid-May
Languages English
Proprietors Rogl family

Tirol

Hotel Restaurant Alpenrose

Kufstein is famous for its Riedel glass factory and, fans would say, the nearby Alpenrose restaurant. The Telser brothers took over their parents' modest guest-house 20 years ago and have built an international reputation for food. Manfred, who trained in Switzerland, is the award-winning chef; his brother, Johann, runs the front-of-house. There are several major companies in town and this is where the executives do business, so the sober, masculine atmosphere of the main dining room is no surprise. Dark wood and brass are softened by gold fabrics; candles gleam against Riedel glassware. Tables in secluded corners are, no doubt, reserved for private conversations.

Waiters whisk in and out with Chef Telser's specialities. These range from local lake fish and simple, grilled sole to a terrine of sweetbreads and venison with Morello cherries. The impressive wine list catalogues some 200 wines from France and Italy as well as Austria. At breakfast, home-made jams and breads are matched by local sausage and ham. Bedrooms suffer by comparison, though the 'new look' in room 109 bodes well for 1994, when refurbishment should be completed.

Nearby Riedel glass factory, winter sports, hiking.

6330 Kufstein, Weissachstr 47
Tel (05372) 62122
Fax (05372) 621227
Location in quiet back street on edge of town; ample car parking
Meals breakfast, lunch, dinner, snacks
Prices rooms AS630-1380 with breakfast; DB&B add AS250; reductions for children; meals from AS255-690
Rooms 22 double, 4 single; all have bath or shower, central heating, phone, TV; most have minibar
Facilities 3 dining-rooms, 2 sitting-rooms, TV room, terrace
Credit Cards MC
Children accepted **Disabled** easy access; lift/elevator
Pets accepted
Closed never
Languages English, French, Italian **Proprietors** Telser brothers

Tirol

❅ **Lakeside hotel, near Lienz** ❅

Parkhotel Tristachersee

Rules are made to be broken. We include the Tristachersee because it is definitely charming and the atmosphere remains 'small' despite the 42 bedrooms. We would happily spend our holiday watching the colours of the lake change a hundred times a day, from brilliant blue in sunshine to soft green in the rain. Every room in the hotel faces either the water or the woods, with not a car in sight.

Josef 'Pepi' Kreuzer began his successful hotel career here 30 years ago and he jumped at the chance of returning to take over the property. That was back in 1987. After a complete face-lift, his meticulous standards have been met. Bedrooms are expensively-furnished, paintings are chosen with care and even the indoor swimming-pool has a mural. All public rooms are large, light and airy, especially the conservatory right on the water. Even the obligatory, wood-panelled *Stube*, named for Emperor Maximilian, who hunted here, is spacious. Food is Pepi's passion, especially fish such as trout, zander and pike which come direct from his latest project, a series of ponds in the garden. This is a sophisticated retreat where luxury is tempered by informality.
Nearby lakes, woods, winter sports, hiking.

9900 Lienz, Tristachersee
Tel (04852) 67666
Fax (04852) 67699
Location on secluded lake; ample car parking
Meals breakfast, lunch, dinner, snacks
Prices rooms AS550-1440 with breakfast; DB&B from AS700-900; reductions for children; meals from AS200
Rooms 32 double, 10 single; all have central heating, phone, TV, radio, hairdrier, safe
Facilities 4 dining-rooms, 2 sitting-rooms, bar, terrace, large indoor swimming-pool, own woods, lake, fishing
Credit Cards not accepted
Children very welcome
Disabled suitable access; lift/ elevator **Pets** accepted
Closed mid-Oct to mid-Dec; restaurant always open
Languages English, French, Italian **Proprietors** Kreuzer family

Tirol

❄ **Apartment hotel, Mayrhofen** ❄

Landhaus Veronika

It is a bold move to go for quality rather than quantity in a resort as popular as Mayrhofen. That, however, is just what Martin and Vroni Huber did when they built their hotel with just nine apartments in 1984. Only 5 minutes' walk from the middle of the village, yet surrounded by fields, the Veronika is "somewhere between a castle and a farmhouse", according to son Bernhard: you have the luxury of the first combined with the cosiness of the second. Family treasures abound: old pictures on the walls; carved figures in niches, and hand-painted targets on the landings.

On one floor, green is the theme colour; on another it is red, but every apartment is different and all reflect Frau Huber's taste. "The advantage we have is that when the weather is poor, guests can use their rooms without feeling cramped." The *Kellerbar* is used for breakfast as well as snacks but no other meals are served. Mayrhofen has plenty of good restaurants, so the Hubers decided not to compete; they do serve breakfast, however, but it is ordered individually rather than taken from a buffet. Some prefer to have breakfast in their apartments, with fresh rolls delivered to their doors.

Nearby Penkenbahn cable car; winter sports; tennis.

6290 Mayrhofen 250b
Tel (05285) 3347
Fax (05285) 3819
Location on edge of village; ample car parking
Meals breakfast, snacks
Prices AS800-2400 for 2, without breakfast
Rooms 9 apartments, all have bath and shower, central heating, phone, TV, minibar, *Kachelofen*
Facilities dining-room, bar; terrace, garden; sauna, whirlpool, solarium
Credit Cards not accepted
Children welcome ·
Disabled not suitable
Pets accepted
Closed never
Languages English, some French
Proprietor Huber family

Tirol

❄ **Modern chalet hotel, near Reutte** ❄

Hotel Fürstenhof

Harti Weirather and Hanni Wenzel were the finest skiers in the world in their heyday and they put the same emphasis on quality when they opened this impressive hotel near the German border. There is carving on the balconies outside and on ceilings and chairs inside. Squashy leather sofas and padded bench seats are designed for comfort. Formerly the Greatlerhof, this peaceful hotel was bought in 1992 by Isabel Kuppelhuber. Every bedroom is a suite, complete with kitchenette, breakfast-table and armchairs for watching television. With its big terrace, broad lawns and tennis courts, the Fürstenhof has the feel of an American country club. Snacks even include a club sandwich and there is spaghetti on the children's menu. Otherwise, the à la carte menu is international, with French onion soup and scampi, as well as Austrian *Schnitzel* and *Käsespätzle*.

Guests are sport and fitness-oriented, so there is a mirror-walled aerobics room plus sauna and steambath in the basement. The Hahnenkamm lift is only 5 minutes' walk away; it may not be as tough as Kitzbühel's; but it was good enough for Harti Weirather to train on; he went on to be world champion in 1982. **Nearby** ski-lift, cross-country trails, tennis, hiking.

6600 Wängle/Holz, Reutte
Tel (05672) 4234
Fax (05672) 423420
Location on hillside in hamlet of Wängle, near Reutte; ample car parking
Meals breakfast, lunch, dinner, snacks
Prices DB&B from AS1140-2500 includes afternoon snack; reductions for children; meals from AS150
Rooms 14 suites; all have bath and shower, central heating, phone, TV, radio
Facilities 3 dining-rooms, sitting-room, bar, TV room, conference room, terrace; fitness facilities
Credit Cards AE, DC
Children very welcome
Disabled not suitable
Pets accepted; not in restaurant **Closed** Nov to mid-Dec; May **Languages** English, Italian **Proprietors** Kuppelhuber family

Tirol

❄ **Modern hotel, Seefeld** ❄

Hotel Prachenskyhof

Imagine a golf-hotel combined with a modern art gallery and you have this four-star hotel set among private houses above Seefeld. The Prachensky family have been architects and painters for 3 generations and 'Prachensky red' is a colour they particularly like, in paintings as much as in carpets. Twenty years ago, this building must have shocked traditionalists, even though the concrete walls are balanced by old wood in the bar, the odd country cupboard, and an ancient metal door leading to the meeting room. There, videos of golfers' games are replayed for analysis by the resident American pro.

At 6 pm the candles are lit in the bar and in the tiny dining-room, where guests sit together, family-style. The ambience is more 'club' than 'hotel' thanks to the common interest in sport: skiing in winter, golf the rest of the year. Even the chef looks suntanned and fit. A few of the 10 bedrooms have galleries for extra space. Generally the decoration is brown wood with white walls and pale blue duvets. Surprisingly, the pale blue bathrooms actually look a little dated. Right outside are the hotel's driving range, putting green and 3 practice holes.

Nearby winter sports, golf, tennis, hiking, fishing.

6100 Seefeld, Panoramaweg
Tel (05212) 27220
Fax (05212) 272256
Location in quiet residential area on edge of Seefeld; ample car parking
Meals breakfast, dinner, snacks
Prices DB&B AS800-2500; reductions for children
Rooms 10 double; all have bath or shower, central heating, phone, TV
Facilities dining-room, sitting-room, bar, TV room, sports and games rooms, sauna, solarium
Credit Cards DC
Children welcome
Disabled suitable access; lift/elevator
Pets accepted
Closed late Oct to mid-Dec; 4 weeks after Easter
Languages English, French, Italian
Proprietors Prachensky family

Tirol

Hotel Viktoria

What do you do if your parents already run a popular hotel in Seefeld like the Veronika? Paul Kirchmair and his wife, Andrea, decided to open somewhere completely different. Where else is there a hotel with themed bedroom suites based on Madison Avenue, La Dolce Vita and Prinz Eugen? Let alone an English butler, Hungarian pictures and Italian chairs? The rotunda-like sitting-room is open-plan. Floor-to-ceiling windows look over the town, glistening wood floors reflect jade-green silk chairs in one corner, big red-black-and-green armchairs stand in another, and there is a chic bar at the back.

The suites, however, are difficult to assess. The background for each is the same: cream walls, big windows, and bold curtains. Our inspectors liked the dramatic '5 Tibetans' suite with its Chinese screen, black lacquer furniture and bold red flower fabric. They hated the Montmartre's chocolate-box pictures of Parisian scenes and were stunned by La Dolce Vita, with its Spanish avant-garde furniture and bold Miró-like colours. Quality abounds but whether you like one of Austria's smallest 5 star hotels or not depends on personal taste.

Nearby winter sports; golf, tennis, hiking.

6100 Seefeld, Geigenbühelweg 589
Tel (05212) 4441
Fax (05212) 4443
Location on edge of town; car parking in underground garage
Meals breakfast, lunch, dinner, snacks
Prices DB&B AS1500-5000 for 2; children up to 16 free in parents' room
Rooms 14 suites; all have bath and shower, central heating, TV, phone, minibar, hairdrier, radio
Facilities dining-room, sitting-room, bar, billiard room, health spa; terrace
Credit Cards AE, DC, MC, V
Children welcome
Disabled easy access; lift/elevator
Pets accepted
Closed 4 weeks after Easter
Languages English, French, Italian
Proprietors Kirchmair family

Tirol

❋ **Mansion hotel, Seefeld** ❋

Wildsee Schlössl

Anna Enn-Schwarz arrived just in time to revive this unusual small hotel on the outskirts of Seefeld. Well-known for its luxury combined with informality, it had begun to fray a little at the edges. Anna bought the Wildsee Schlössl from her brother in May 1992 and enthusiastically set about restoring its reputation.

Most guests take half-board, and are rarely disappointed by Christian Suitner's cooking. 'It is good Austrian cooking; a little bit nouvelle, but basically authentic Viennese cuisine.' So *carpaccio* might be followed by vegetable soup and salad from the buffet. Choose between loin of veal or venison with wild mushrooms and potato strudel and follow that with plums in an almond sauce. Frau Schwarz's brother, Ferdinand Enn, won Austria's prestigious 'Waiter of the Year' title a decade ago.

The bedrooms are in different shapes and sizes, up steps, round corners and down corridors. Room 302 has the circular tower, where guests like to watch the sun set. Room 202 opens on to the garden and is particularly popular with the ever-increasing number of golfers who enjoy both the special rates and the proximity of the course.

Nearby golf, tennis, swimming; winter sports.

6100 Seefeld, Innsbruckerstr 195
Tel (05212) 2390
Fax (05212) 239012
Location on approach to Seefeld, by Wildmoossee; public car parking across street
Meals breakfast, lunch, dinner
Prices DB&B AS925-1200; reductions for children; meals from AS300
Rooms 18 double, 2 single; all have bath or shower, central heating, phone, TV, radio
Facilities 3 dining-rooms, sitting-room, bar; terrace, garden; sauna, steam bath
Credit Cards AE, DC, MC, V
Children very welcome
Disabled not suitable
Pets accepted
Closed Nov; April; check with hotel
Languages some English, French, Italian
Proprietors Schwarz family

Tirol

Restaurant with rooms, Zirl

Hotel Goldener Löwe

Zirl is a small town, just off the motorway west of Innsbruck. The Goldener Löwe is arguably its main attraction. Businessmen flock here to eat; children are enchanted by the pony-sized, stuffed brown bear in the entrance hall and delight in riding on its back. The Plattner family have owned the inn for generations, but when Otto Plattner recently took over the Europa Hotel in Innsbruck, he left his daughter and son-in-law, Andreas Liepert, in charge.

When our inspectors arrived some diners were tucking into a delicate terrine of trout or spinach fritters, followed by a mixed grill of both freshwater and sea fish or the traditional *Tafelspitz*. Desserts were tempting: a white chocolate mousse with mocha sauce and poppy-seed pancakes with rum cream.

Nearly half the bedrooms are singles, emphasizing the number of guests who are on business. Padded leather doors are studded; inside, trouser presses stand waiting. Slowly the rooms are being refurbished. The *Appartments* are particularly impressive with plenty of sitting space, complete with large armchairs. The bathrooms have grey-veined marble and whirlpool baths.

Nearby Fragenstein castle; Telfs; Innsbruck.

6170 Zirl
Tel (05238) 2330
Fax (05238) 263138
Location in middle of town; car parking at rear
Meals breakfast, lunch, dinner, snacks
Prices AS625-1300 with breakfast; DB&B from AS875; meals from AS190
Rooms 9 double, 11 single, 8 suite; all have bath or shower, central heating, phone, TV, minibar; some air-conditioning, hairdrier
Facilities 3 dining-rooms, bar; sauna
Credit Cards AE, DC, MC, V
Children welcome
Disabled access via lift/elevator at rear
Pets accepted
Closed 6 Jan to 1 Feb
Languages English
Proprietors Plattner-Liepert family

Tirol

❄   Resort hotel, Berwang   ❄

Edelweiss

By building on a semi-circular dining room, the Sprengers have made their Tyrolean-style hotel bright and welcoming. Sauna, whirlpool. Three ski-lifts are within walking distance. Slopes ideal for beginners and low-intermediates.

■ 6622 Berwang **Tel** (05674) 84230 **Fax** (05674) 842329 **Meals** breakfast, lunch, dinner, snacks **Prices** rooms AS325-1200 with breakfast **Rooms** 19, all with bath or shower, central heating, phone, radio **Credit cards** not accepted **Closed** Oct to mid-Dec; after Easter to early June **Languages** English

❄   Old inn, Ebbs   ❄

Hotel Unterwirt

The Steindl's hotel is in the middle of Ebbs, a small Tyrolean village known for its summer concerts and Haflinger horses. The Unterwirt, with its decorated windows, is best known for its light, regional dishes served in an authentic *Stube*.

■ 6341 Ebbs **Tel** (05373) 2288 **Fax** (05373) 2253 **Meals** breakfast, lunch, dinner, snacks **Prices** rooms AS350-720 with breakfast **Rooms** 29, all with bath or shower, central heating, phone, TV, radio **Credit cards** not accepted **Closed** Nov to mid-Dec; 1 week after Easter **Languages** English, French, some Spanish

❄   Resort hotel, Fügen   ❄

Hotel Haidachhof

This standard, chalet-style, modern hotel is surprisingly luxurious inside with an indoor swimming-pool and à la carte restaurant. Gretl Heim's warm welcome and the nearby Spieljoch lift ensure a regular flow of both families and couples.

■ 6263 Fügen, Hochfügenerstr 280 **Tel** (05288) 2380 **Fax** (05288) 338866 **Meals** breakfast, lunch, dinner, snacks **Prices** rooms AS350-1200 with breakfast **Rooms** 28, all with bath, shower, central heating, phone, TV **Credit cards** not accepted **Closed** Nov to mid-Dec; 1 week after Easter **Languages** English, some Italian

❄   Town hotel, Fulpmes   ❄

Hotel-Garni Hubertus

Regular skiers from as far afield as the USA and Holland are pleased to see the face-lift for this informal, turn-of-the-century bed-and-breakfast that overlooks the bandstand. Sound value, with indoor swimming-pool, sauna. Skiing on Stubai Glacier.

■ 6166 Fulpmes, Medrazerstr 20 **Tel** (05225) 2294 **Meals** breakfast **Prices** rooms AS295-800 with breakfast **Rooms** 27, all with shower, central heating, radio **Credit cards** not accepted **Closed** never **Languages** some English

Tirol

❈   Chalet hotel, Fulpmes   ❈

Hotel Atzinger

Located in Medraz, on the edge of Fulpmes. Facilities are right
up-to-date, including a solarium and children's playroom. The
Atzinger family make a point of using local products – eggs,
milk, butter and cheese. Value for family holidays.
■ 6166 Fulpmes, Sonnegg 22 **Tel** (05225) 3135 **Fax** (05225) 3135134
Meals breakfast, lunch, dinner, snacks **Prices** rooms AS320-1150 with
breakfast **Rooms** 30, all with bath or shower, central heating, phone, TV
Credit cards not accepted **Closed** Nov to mid-Dec; 4 weeks after
Easter **Languages** English

❈   Country inn, Gnadenwald   ❈

Alpenhotel Speckbacher

Good food and informality attract both holidaymakers and locals
from Innsbruck to this expanded inn. Children swim in the
pond, parents relax in the garden. Dark country furniture,
simple rooms. Useful base for walking and cross-country skiing.
■ 6060 Gnadenwald, St. Martin **Tel** (05223) 2511 **Fax** (05223) 251155
Meals breakfast, lunch, dinner, snacks **Prices** rooms AS360-1100 with
breakfast **Rooms** 19, all with bath or shower, central heating, phone;
most with TV **Credit cards** AE, DC, MC, V **Closed** Nov; 2 weeks after
Easter **Languages** English, French, Italian

❈   Country guest-house, Hinterriss   ❈

Herzoglicher Alpenhof

In one of Tyrol's prettiest valleys, this rustic hotel needs no frills
to attract guests to the Karwendel conservation area. Open fires,
red-and-white-checked duvets and farmhouse food keep hikers
happy in summer, cross-country skiers in winter.
■ 6200 Hinterriss **Tel** (05245) 207 **Fax** (05245) 20711 **Meals** breakfast,
lunch, dinner, snacks **Prices** rooms AS300-700 with breakfast **Rooms**
20, all with bath or shower, central heating, phone **Credit cards** not
accepted **Closed** Nov to mid-Dec; April to mid-May **Languages**
English, Italian

❈   Resort hotel, Igls   ❈

Hotel Ägidihof

Upgraded, but retaining a traditional look, this inn has plain
wood panelling, rustic furniture in the *Tiroler Stube,* deep armchairs in the sitting areas and an international menu. Five minutes from ski-lifts, Kurpark, tennis, and golf driving range.
■ 6080 Igls, Lanserstr **Tel** (0512) 77108 **Fax** (0512) 771086 **Meals**
breakfast, lunch, dinner, snacks **Prices** rooms AS450-2000 with
breakfast **Rooms** 28, all with bath or shower, central heating, phone; TV
on request **Credit cards** AE, DC, MC, V **Closed** mid-Oct to early Dec
Languages English

Tirol

❊   Resort hotel, Igls   ❊

Hotel Alt Igls

This solid, attractive hotel in the middle of the village was renovated in 1978, so the dark brown beam-and-leather look remains. The terrace, café and bar are popular meeting spots. Unusually, the indoor swimming-pool is on the top floor.

■ 6080 Igls, Hilberstr 3 **Tel** (0512) 78133 **Fax** (0512) 781335 **Meals** breakfast, lunch, dinner, snacks **Prices** rooms AS650-1300 with breakfast **Rooms** 30, all with bath or shower, central heating, phone, TV, radio, safe **Credit cards** MC, V **Closed** early Oct to mid-Dec; after Easter to early May **Languages** English, French, Italian

---

❊   Historic inn, Innsbruck   ❊

Romantikhotel Schwarzer Adler

Famous? Yes. Cosy? Yes. Romantic? Maybe. This 400-year-old institution desperately needs a facelift. The restaurant, with its low arches, still pulls in locals and tourists for regional dishes and impressive wines, but the bedrooms and public areas are dowdy.

■ 6020 Innsbruck, Universitätstr **Tel** (0512) 587109 **Fax** (0512) 561697 **Meals** breakfast, lunch, dinner, snacks **Prices** rooms AS750-1900 with breakfast **Rooms** 26, with bath or shower, central heating, phone, TV, radio, minibar, hairdrier **Credit cards** AE, DC, MC, V **Closed** never; restaurant only, Sun **Languages** English, French, Italian

---

❊   Resort hotel, Kitzbühel   ❊

Hotel Resch

Don't be put off by the busy Wienerwald café at street-level. The Resch has comfy seats in the sitting areas and a pretty, pale blue restaurant. Quieter rooms are at the back. The bonus is nearness both to the Hahnenkamm cable car (4 min) and the Aquarena.

■ 6370 Kitzbühel, Petzoldweg **Tel** (05356) 2294 **Fax** (05356) 5006 **Meals** breakfast, lunch, dinner, snacks **Prices** rooms AS450-1500 with breakfast **Rooms** 22, all with bath or shower, central heating, phone, TV **Credit cards** AE, DC, MC, V **Closed** mid-Oct to 1 Dec; mid-April to mid-May **Languages** English, French, Italian

---

❊   New hotel, Kufstein   ❊

Lanthalerhof

Built in the traditional style, this new hotel is lavish with marble as well as heavily-carved, pale wood panelling. Bedrooms are white, with soft greys and reds; the garden is peaceful. Near the Riedel glass factory. Own ski-bus to Schiwelt-Söll.

■ 6330 Kufstein, Schopperweg 28 **Tel** (05372) 64105 **Meals** breakfast, lunch, dinner, snacks **Prices** rooms AS330-800 with breakfast **Rooms** 20, all with bath or shower, central heating, phone, TV, radio **Credit cards** not accepted **Closed** never **Languages** German only

Tirol

❋   Resort hotel, Lermoos   ❋

Silence-Sporthotel Zugspitze

With yellow umbrellas on the terrace and the Zugspitze Mountains in the background, the temptation is to sit and do nothing at this secluded hotel. However, Irena Scheiderbauer organizes cycling tours and torch-lit tobogganing. Near Hochmoos ski-lift.
■ 6631 Lermoos, Innsbruckerstr 51 **Tel** (05673) 2630 **Fax** (05673) 263015 **Meals** breakfast, lunch, dinner, snacks **Prices** rooms AS590-1500 with breakfast **Rooms** 26, all with bath or shower, central heating, phone, TV, radio **Credit cards** not accepted **Closed** mid-Oct to mid-Dec; 4 weeks after Easter **Languages** English, Italian

---

❋   Village inn, Matrei in Osttirol   ❋

Hotel Panzlwirt

The Panzl family tree, painted outside, goes back to 1786, so we expected tradition, not the jade green, steel and wood bar where locals mix with guests back from skiing the Goldried slopes. Bedrooms are comfortable if unremarkable. Good for families.
■ 9971 Matrei in Osttirol, Tauerntalstr 4 **Tel** (04875) 6518 **Fax** (04875) 65188 **Meals** breakfast, lunch, dinner, snacks **Prices** rooms AS295-1290; meals from AS100 **Rooms** 14, all with bath or shower, central heating, phone, TV, radio **Credit cards** not accepted **Closed** never **Languages** English, Italian

---

❋   Resort hotel, Mutters   ❋

Hotel Sonnhof

Marianne Ullman's modern hotel offers above-average comfort and is ideal for families with small children, thanks to a large garden, a proper indoor swimming-pool and nearby skiing. Only a 5-minute walk to the middle of the village.
■ 6162 Mutters, Burgstall 12 **Tel** (0512) 573747 **Fax** (0512) 584500 **Meals** breakfast, lunch, dinner, snacks **Prices** rooms AS425-1400 with breakfast **Rooms** 28, all with bath or shower, central heating, phone, TV, radio **Credit cards** not accepted **Closed** mid-Oct to mid-Dec; after Easter to early May **Languages** English, Italian

---

❋   Old inn, Nassereith   ❋

Hotel Schloss Fernsteinsee

Mad King Ludwig of Bavaria loved the brilliant green Fernsteinsee lake. He would also love this eccentric hotel, on a sharp bend in the road. The outrageous marble and gilt fittings extend even to the lavatories. Not to everyone's taste.
■ 6465 Nassereith **Tel** (05265) 5210 **Fax** (05265) 52174 **Meals** breakfast, lunch, dinner, snacks **Prices** rooms AS450-1500 with breakfast **Rooms** 25, all with bath or shower, central heating, phone, TV **Credit cards** not accepted **Closed** Nov to mid-Dec; mid-Jan to mid-Feb **Languages** English

Tirol

❋　Village inn, Oetz　❋

Gasthof Zum Stern

Oetz is full of painted houses and the Griessers' 12thC inn is no exception. Add an unusual oriel window over the entrance, wood panelling, solid oak tables and chairs in the dining-rooms and you can forgive the plastic in the bathrooms.

■ 6433 Oetz, Kirchweg 6 **Tel** (05252) 6323 **Fax** same **Meals** breakfast, lunch, dinner **Prices** rooms AS280-460 with breakfast; meals AS120-150 **Rooms** 14, all with shower **Credit Cards** not accepted **Closed** never **Languages** some English

---

❋　Resort hotel, St Anton am Arlberg　❋

St Antoner Hof

Fun, Tyrolean-style, with an indoor pool, jazz piano and new Austrian cooking as well as old beams, painted furniture and four-poster beds. This is where affluent young skiers come for the mixture of luxury and tradition.

■ 6580 St Anton am Arlberg **Tel** (05446) 2910 **Fax** (05446) 3551 **Meals** breakfast, lunch, dinner, snacks **Prices** rooms AS680-1600 with breakfast **Rooms** 31, all with bath or shower, central heating, phone, TV, radio, safe **Credit cards** DC, MC, V **Closed** Nov to mid-Dec; after Easter to mid-June **Languages** English, French, Italian

---

❋　Resort hotel, Seefeld　❋

Hotel Garni Almhof

The Reindl family took a lot of trouble over this attractive chalet, built on the edge of Seefeld in 1989. The new wood is heavily carved, fabrics are in soft, warm shades. 3 minutes from Geigenbühel ski area, tennis courts. Own cabin on nearby lake.

■ 6100 Seefeld, Geigenbühelstr 746 **Tel** (05212) 3066 **Fax** (05212) 306651 **Meals** breakfast, snacks **Prices** rooms AS370-1100 **Rooms** 14, all with bath or shower, central heating, phone, TV, radio; some with kitchenette **Credit card** V **Closed** mid-Oct to mid-Dec; early April to early June **Languages** English

---

❋　Village inn, Strassen　❋

Strasserwirt

A classic 350-year old inn in a tiny, unspoilt village on the sunny side of the Hochpustertal valley in East Tyrol. The Bürglers offer everything from breakfast in the forest to yoga courses and cross-country skiing. Downhill skiing at Thurntaler ski area (5 km).

■ 9920 Strassen **Tel** (04846) 6354 **Fax** (04846) 635455 **Meals** breakfast, lunch, dinner, snacks **Prices** rooms AS410-1800 with breakfast **Rooms** 28, all with bath or shower, central heating, phone, TV, radio, safe **Credit cards** MC, V **Closed** Nov to mid-Dec; 2 weeks after Easter **Languages** English, French, Italian

Salzburgerland

Hotels in Salzburgerland

Salzburg and its state have both a rich landscape and a rich history. Mozart is virtually synonymous with the old city which celebrates its love of the arts during the annual Festival. All around are mountains and lakes, perfect for skiing and sailing.

With its thundering waterfall, Badgastein has always been a well-known resort. Hidden in a quiet valley round the corner is the excellent Hotel Grüner Baum which is more like a small village than hotel. The Blumschein family are outstanding hoteliers (Tel (06434) 25160, fax 251625, 91 rooms). Guests go home with the hotel's own chocolate cake packed in a small wooden box.

Further down the valley, in Bad Hofgastein, is Zum Toni, a jolly hotel dedicated to skiing, eating and fun with the Pichler family who also have their own mountain hut (Tel (06432) 6629, fax 662933, 20 rooms).

Another winter sports destination is Flachau where Erika Kohlmayr's Hotel Felsenhof is both comfortable and intimate and therefore gets many regulars (Tel (06457) 2251, fax 267610, 30 rooms).

Maria Alm boasts the highest spire in the state as well as spectacular scenery near the Steinernes Meer mountains. The Pension Dreimäderlhaus is a simple, yet ideal place to explore the town, ski or hike (Tel (06584) 7409, 10 rooms).

It is not necessary to stay in Salzburg to enjoy the city. All around the Trumer lakes to the north, a mere 20 minutes' drive away, are a host of cheerful hotels. We are watching the progress of the Richter family who have recently taken over the Bräugasthof Sigl in Obertrum. This cavernous old edifice should soon be upgraded with better quality rooms (Tel (06219) 7700, fax 741133, 20 rooms). Meanwhile we are happy to sit out under the chestnut trees to enjoy Herr Sigl's outstanding beer from the ancient brewery across the street.

Nearby, in Seeham, the Hotel Walkner has a secluded garden and swimming-pool, overlooking the lake (Tel (06217) 550, fax 55022, 22 rooms).

Across in St Michael in Lungau, well-known as a spa and ski-resort, is the comfortable Staigerwirt run by Michael Gruber (Tel (06477) 206, 10 rooms).

For further details about the area, contact:
Salzburger Land – Tourismus Ges m.b.H,
Alpenstrasse 96,
A-5033 Salzburg
Tel: (0662) 205060
Fax: (0662) 23070

This page acts as an introduction to the features and hotels of Salzburgerland and gives brief recommendations of good hotels that for one reason or another have not made a full entry. The long entries for this state – covering the hotels we are most enthusiastic about – start on the next page. But do not neglect the shorter entries starting on page 81: these are all hotels that we would happily stay at.

Salzburgerland

Hotel-Restaurant Lebzelter

In the past 5 years, the small town of Altenmarkt has become a more attractive base for skiers using the Zauchensee area thanks to a complete face-lift. The hotel that has benefitted most is the Lebzelter. Now it stands in a pedestrian zone and it, too, has been renovated completely.

Big straw dolls guard the restaurant entrance. Inside, the arched ceilings, butter-yellow tablecloths and quarry tile floor prove that old buildings can be updated without losing their character.

As for food, choose from hearty Pongau recipes featuring local Taurach trout and Tauern lamb, the health-conscious daily *Vitalmenu* and 'new Austrian' dishes.

Upstairs, bedrooms have a bright, almost American look with bold flowery curtains, matching sofas and bedspreads, all set against cream and pink walls. Bathrooms are in practical white tiles. Some traditions, however, continue. The church bells ring out at 6 am, so rooms at the rear are advised.

Mountain bikes are available and the Kohlmayrs take guests out to their mountain hut in summer for dinner and music. **Nearby** winter sports, walking, old town.

5541 Altenmarkt 79
Tel (06452) 6911
Fax (06452) 7823
Location in middle of town, in pedestrian zone; car parking at side of hotel
Meals breakfast, lunch, dinner, snacks
Prices AS500-1800 with breakfast; DB&B from AS565; reduction for children; meals from AS200
Rooms 26 double, one single, 2 suites; all have bath or shower, central heating, phone, TV, minibar, hairdrier, radio **Facilities** 3 dining-rooms, bar, table-tennis room, terrace, saunas with solarium
Credit Cards AE, DC, MC, V
Children very welcome
Disabled very accessible, especially Room 108
Pets accepted (AS70 per day)
Closed never **Languages** English, French, Italian, Spanish **Proprietors** Kohlmayr family

Salzburgerland

❄   **Spa hotel, Badgastein**   ❄

Haus Hirt

Wedged high above Badgastein, the 70-year old building looks a little dour as you drive up the Kaiserpromenade. Any misgivings, however, are dispelled immediately by big vases of fresh flowers, Persian carpets on parquet floors, armchairs that look inviting and views northwest over the Gastein Valley.

Kurt Raschhofer's hobby is interior decorating and he loves English fabrics, hence the deep gold William Morris print on the chaise longue in room 57. Some bedrooms are split-level, with a sitting room downstairs and the bed and bathroom upstairs. In fact, the number of rooms here is actually decreasing as bedrooms and bathrooms are enlarged.

Throughout, the traditional blends with the modern. The Biedermeier Room has a piano, library and cupboard full of games but the broad, low-level bar with leather swivel chairs looks strictly 1990s.

The breakfast buffet is particularly impressive, with 14 herbal teas, half a dozen home-made jams and bread so delicious that guests often take a loaf home. In the basement is a fully-equipped health farm complete with consultant doctor.

Nearby winter sports, walking, casino.

5640 Badgastein, Kaiserpromenade
Tel (06434) 2797
Fax (06434) 279748
Location on steep road above town; 4 garages
Meals breakfast, dinner, snacks
Prices AS750-1800 with breakfast; DB&B from AS750; reduction for children
Rooms 8 double, 4 single, 13 suites; all have bath and shower, central heating, phone, TV, minibar, hairdrier, safe, trouser press
Facilities dining-room, 4 sitting-rooms, bar, TV room, terrace, health farm, heated pool **Credit Cards** AE, DC, MC, V **Children** welcome
Disabled accessible via lift/ elevator **Pets** accepted
Closed April to mid-May; mid-Oct to mid-Dec
Languages English, French, Italian, Dutch **Proprietors** Raschhofer family

Salzburgerland

❊ **Converted villa, Badgastein** ❊

Villa Solitude

Back in 1838, this idyllic villa was the only building overlooking the famous Gastein falls. Surprisingly, it still offers peace and quiet, despite being on the main road and next door to the casino, since all six bedrooms are at the back, looking over the valley. In 1990, the Blumschein family rescued this minor treasure and recreated the romance of the 19thC with antiques and silk fabrics.

Each room reflects a previous owner or visitor. The Kaiserin Sissy Suite has a double bed tucked into a panelled alcove; the Kaiser Wilhelm Suite retains the original large, square, wooden floor tiles but now sunshine-yellow curtains frame the tall French windows. A small breakfast room and library with fireplace complete this tiny time-machine.

Having restored the old, the Blumschein's installed the new. Rooms have fax sockets and satellite TV; bathrooms are regal, with the ribbon-and-tassle motif repeated on thick dressing gowns. Guests are encouraged to use the excellent Brasserie restaurant next door and the swimming and health facilities at the Grüner Baum hotel – both owned by the Blumscheins.

Nearby Casino, winter sports, walking

5640 Badgastein, Kaiser Franz Joseph Str 16
Tel (06434) 51010
Fax (06434) 51013
Location in middle of Badgastein, overlooking falls; car parking outside, 3 garages
Meals breakfast
Prices AS2000-3000 with breakfast; DB&B from AS2300
Rooms 5 double, 1 suite with 2 double rooms; all have bath and shower, central heating, phone, TV, minibar, hairdrier, fax point, safe, trouser press
Facilities terrace, small library; sports and health facilities at Grüner Baum
Credit Cards AE, DC, MC, V
Children accepted but not very suitable **Disabled** not suitable **Pets** not accepted
Closed May, Nov; restaurant only, Sun **Languages** English, French, Italian **Proprietors** Blumschein family; Manager, Frau Widder

Salzburgerland

❄ **Mountain village hotel, Filzmoos** ❄

Hotel Hubertus

Filzmoos is a busy village at the foot of the Bischofsmütze and Dachstein Massif. Right in the middle is the Hubertus which has evolved from grandpa's ordinary guest-house to a modern, angular hotel where, since 1991, the Art Deco-influenced purple and white gourmet restaurant has been a showcase for Johanna Maier's outstanding cooking. The rest of the ground floor is open-plan, with big windows in the informal restaurant, patronised by walkers and skiers. Above, rooms are a fresh-looking combination of pale pine, white walls and green carpets with glassed-in balconies.

This is very much a family enterprise. Dietmar Maier produces an excellent wine list of international vintages and also teaches fly-fishing on the nearby lakes and rivers. Eldest son Tobias is up early to bake breakfast rolls (the hazelnut are especially good) while the youngest son was observed stealing a slice of chocolate cake on his way to school. The 8-course gourmet dinner on Thursday is excellent value, as are the winter ski-breaks which include lift passes. Our inspector's final memory is of Johanna's rhubarb ice cream – 'the best she'd ever tasted'.

Nearby winter sports, walking, fishing.

5532 Filzmoos, Am Dorfplatz
Tel (06453) 204
Fax (06453) 2066
Location in middle of village; car parking in own garage
Meals breakfast, lunch, dinner, snacks
Prices AS430-1260 with breakfast; DB&B from AS550; meals from AS200
Rooms 9 double, 2 single, 4 family, with bunk beds in separate rooms; all have bath or shower, central heating, phone, TV
Facilities 2 dining-rooms, bar, terrace, sauna, solarium, steam bath
Credit Cards not accepted
Children very welcome
Disabled lift/elevator, Room 11 suitable
Pets accepted
Closed end-April to mid-May; Nov to mid-Dec
Languages English, French, Italian, some Dutch
Proprietors Maier family

Salzburgerland

Hotel Seehof

Goldegg is a village of preserved old houses, restored cobbled streets and no modern development. This large white inn is 500 years old. Three chestnut trees shade the entrance which leads straight into a comfortable sitting area and bar. Guests stretch out on bench seats with a novel from the bookcase or chat in the cosily-grouped armchairs. Informal enough for children to relax, it is nice enough for them to mind their manners.

Watercolours line the walls and a large battleflag hangs above the stairs which creak as you go up to the rooms. Five have blue-painted peasant furniture but all have white walls with flowery curtains and cheerful red and green cushions. "It has been an inn since 1727 and we're the fourth generation of Schellhorns to run it," says Karola who was the chef for 20 years. Now her son, Sepp, is in charge, producing gossamer-thin strudel pastry to envelope apple or rhubarb. Father Franz leads guests on cross-country or downhill ski safaris. There is also ice-skating and curling on the frozen lake which, in summer, is perfect for swimming.

Nearby old village, castle, winter sports, lake, walking, 9 hole golf course.

5622 Goldegg am See
Tel (06415) 81370
Fax (06415) 8276
Location at end of village, overlooking the lake; car parking beside hotel
Meals breakfast, lunch, dinner, snacks
Prices DB&B AS760-900; reduction for children; meals from AS150
Rooms 18 double, 7 single, 2 family; all have bath or shower, central heating, phone, TV; some radios, safes
Facilities dining-room, 3 sitting areas, bar, games room, terrace, sauna, steam bath
Credit Cards DC, V
Children very welcome
Disabled not suitable
Pets accepted (AS 100)
Closed April; Nov
Languages English
Proprietors Schellhorn family

Salzburgerland

Converted brewery, Mattsee

Iglhauser Bräu

The current owner of this imposing hotel is the fifth Jakob Iglhauser; his son, who is training to join the business, is Jakob VI. The Iglhausers, however, account for only a fraction of the history of the premises. Hospitality has been dispensed here since 1200, and although the hostelry and brew-house of long ago were much simpler, the bustle of activity was much the same. Waiters hurry from the kitchen past the reception desk and into the dining-rooms: one decorated with murals and a collection of pewterware; another, less formal, with bench seats and *Kachelofen*.

Frau Iglhauser is in charge of the kitchen and it is her collection of dolls that welcomes visitors in the entrance hall. Bedrooms have white walls and forest-green fabrics that set off ancient beams and floors. Bathrooms are up-do-date, however, and there are even a few four-poster beds. The Iglhausers are enthusiastic hoteliers, adding new bedrooms and hosting seminars and weddings. Guests are encouraged to use the hotel's own sailing dinghies, rowing boats and windsurfing boards. Not the place for complete relaxation, perhaps, but fun for children and with Salzburg half an hour away, handy enough for city visits.

Nearby lake, watersports; Buchberg National Park; Salzburg.

5163 Mattsee, Schlossbergweg 4
Tel (06217) 205
Fax (06217) 20533
Location on edge of town, on lake Mattsee; car parking around hotel, garage
Meals breakfast, lunch, dinner, snacks
Prices AS600-2400; meals from AS200
Rooms 20 double, all with bath or shower; all have phone, central heating, TV, hairdrier
Facilities 3 dining-rooms, conference and banqueting facilities; terrace; free watersports
Credit Cards MC, V
Children very welcome
Disabled not suitable
Pets accepted
Closed 2 weeks end Oct
Languages English
Proprietors Iglhauser family

Salzburgerland

Nationalparkhotel Felben

We are rarely impressed by brand-new hotels but this is an exception. Surrounded on three sides by fields but close enough to walk into the village, the Scharler family's 1989-vintage hotel is next to the cleanest farmyard we have ever seen. Cows, chickens and horses delight the children of parents who, understandably, book up early to stay here. Bedrooms are big enough for boisterous families, with attractive pink duvets, pale mauve carpets and solid wood furniture. The attention to detail deserves applause for the baby-changing facilities outside the basement lavatories and the provision of crayons and paper in the vaulted dining room. There are no compromises, however, on the food, which includes home-made jams, cheeses and even herbal teas. Half-board guests are offered a choice of meat, fish or vegetarian dishes.

The emphasis here is on health and fitness, with non-smoking bedrooms and restaurant areas and a swimming-pool heated year-round. Gunter, the fitness expert and ski instructor, leads the programme of activities for children, summer and winter.

Nearby Hohe Tauern National Park, museum, winter sports, riding, walking.

5730 Mittersill
Tel (06562) 4407
Fax (06562) 478572
Location in village of Felben, on edge of Mittersill; car parking outside hotel
Meals breakfast, lunch, dinner, snacks
Prices DB&B AS690-800; reduction for children
Rooms 28 double, 3 suites, all with bath or shower; all have central heating, phone, TV, minibar, safe

Facilities 3 dining rooms, bar, games rooms, terraces, garden, health and fitness centre, heated swimming-pool
Credit Cards not accepted
Children especially welcome
Disabled not suitable
Pets not accepted
Closed Nov to mid-Dec; after Easter to Ascension
Languages English
Proprietors Franz and Barbara Scharler

Salzburgerland

Country inn, Anif near Salzburg

Romantik Hotel Schlosswirt

This is where locals bring their out-of-town friends to show them a typical, old Salzburgerland inn. When the Grafs took over the guesthouse of the nearby castle back in 1962 they were determined to "put the soul back in the building." They also decided to leave the austere, tunnel-like entrance hall rather than alter the architecture unnecessarily. Wooden benches in the *Bierstüberl* date from 1607, with antlers and a grandfather clock for decoration. The dining-rooms look turn-of-the-century with dark green walls, wood floors and old oil paintings.

The sense of history persists upstairs where framed pages of 19thC magazines about hunting and mountaineering hang on the walls. Each bedroom is different: number 5 has a plaid pink and red theme, number 8 has butter yellow and green fabrics, and number 17 boasts a large sleigh bed and overlooks the stream and garden at the back. "We never wanted a fancy hotel," insists Heimo Graf. "Even our food is strictly traditional though the quality has risen in 20 years." Across the street the 15thC Kramerbauer annexe also has comfortable rooms with balconies.

Nearby Salzburg 20 minutes, tennis, golf.

5081 Anif bei Salzburg
Tel (06246) 2175
Fax (06246) 217580
Location on main road, on outskirts of Anif; ample car parking
Meals breakfast, lunch, dinner, snacks
Prices AS670-1800 with breakfast; extra bed in room AS300; meals from AS150
Rooms 22 double, 7 single; all have bath or shower, central heating, phone

Facilities 3 dining rooms, sitting-room/TV room, bar, terrace
Credit Cards AE, DC, MC, V
Children welcome
Disabled suitable
Pets accepted (AS 60)
Closed Feb
Languages English
Proprietors Heimo and Hannelore Graf

Salzburgerland

Country inn, Salzburg-Elixhausen

Romantik Hotel Gmachl

The outside of this classic country inn cannot have changed much since the first Gmachls moved here back in 1583. The inside, however, saw a major overhaul in 1987. White walls and moss-green bench seats show off the pale, old wood in the reception area while dried flowers are outnumbered by old prints. The *Kaiserzimmer,* the original tavern, is now a restaurant where diners duck through a low, carved wooden doorway. The less formal *Gaststube* has big tables and a bottle-green *Kachelofen* covered in biblical scenes.

Upstairs, the ancient rooms have been sensitively refurbished with TV sets banished to cabinets. Across the street, a converted barn provides 22 new bedrooms, all in cool combinations of peach, green and yellow.

All the Gmachls are involved. Fritz's *Metzgerei (*butcher's) provides villagers as well as guests with his famous *Bratwurst;* rosettes confirm the showjumping skills of his daughters who help entertain children at the nearby stables during the holidays. There is a terrace garden and a swimming pool but best of all, the young staff really seem to enjoy working here.

Nearby riding, tennis, Salzburg (20 minutes).

5161 Salzburg-Elixhausen
Tel (0662) 58212
Fax (0662) 5857272
Location in middle of village; car parking outside hotel
Meals breakfast, lunch, dinner, snacks
Prices AS660-2400 with breakfast; reduction for children; extra bed in room AS250; meals from AS250
Rooms 6 single, 6 suites, with 4 beds, plus 22 double in annexe; all have bath or shower, central heating, phone, TV, radio; some hairdriers **Facilities** 3 dining-rooms, bar, terrace, garden, outdoor pool
Credit Cards not accepted
Children very welcome
Disabled not suitable
Pets accepted **Closed** 14 to 28 June; restaurant only, Sun, Mon **Languages** English, French, some Italian
Proprietors Fritz and Theresia Gmachl

Salzburgerland

❅ **Chalet hotel, Salzburg (Elsbethen)** ❅

Hotel Schwaitlalm

The road from Glasenbach leads up switchbacks through dense woods and then, suddenly, into alpine meadows. This shingled farmhouse is over 400 years old but the hunting lodge next door is even older.

Lucia and Domenico Birenti took over the property in 1991 and have redecorated about half of the rooms, changing the older, darker colours for paler tones and unusual patterned fabrics. "I don't like the old rooms but lots of guests do," Lucia Birenti told us, "so I'll have to leave one as it is".

Downstairs, the *Stube* has cornflower-blue table cloths and curtains with framed hand-written recipes from an old book on the walls. The dining-room is more formal but also has views south across the valley to the hills of Germany. The menu, like the Birenti family, is Austro-Italian, with carpaccio and ravioli, *Tafelspitz* and *Topfenknödel*.

Despite its rural setting, the hotel is only 15 minutes from Salzburg and 5 minutes from the Gaisberg ski area. Popular with families as well as overseas visitors, it has tennis courts, a large indoor pool and sauna/solarium.

Nearby winter sports; hiking trails; Salzburg.

5061 Elsbethen bei Salzburg
Tel (0662) 25927
Fax (0662) 296063
Location in hills near Salzburg; ample car parking
Meals breakfast, lunch, dinner, snacks
Prices rooms AS850-1600 with breakfast; reduction for children; meals from AS100
Rooms 14 double, 3 suites; all have bath or shower, central heating, phone, TV, minibar, radio

Facilities dining-room, terrace, sauna, solarium, indoor heated pool
Credit Cards not accepted
Children very welcome
Disabled access to restaurant, not rooms
Pets accepted
Closed early Jan to early March
Languages English, Italian
Proprietors Lucia and Domenico Birenti

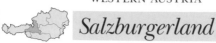

Salzburgerland

Converted mansion, Salzburg-Parsch

Hotel Fondachhof

This still feels like the private home it was until the present owner's father turned it into a first-class hotel some 40 years ago. Once inside the impressive gates, Salzburg and its suburbs seem far away. With extensive lawns, rose garden, gravel paths and rhododendrons, fans of English country house hotels will feel right at home. They can even have eggs for breakfast, though other tastes are satisfied with croissants and *Speck,* muesli and home-made jams. Taken outside, with views of the Kreuzberg mountain, this is a delightful start to the day.

The house dates back 350 years, so rooms come in all shapes and sizes. The decoration in each is different, ranging from number 19, an enormous double featuring an 18thC sleigh bed with inlaid wood, to number 10, a cozy single with early 19thC painted *Bauern* bed and sideboard. The family collection of antiques is worth studying: here a 1792 calendar, there a Chinese vase. There is also a separate annexe with bedrooms decorated in pretty floral prints, a summer house for private parties and a swimming pool. No wonder this is a retreat for celebrities during the Festival.

Nearby Gaisberg, Kapuzinerberg; Salzburg.

5020 Salzburg-Parsch, Gaisbergstr 46
Tel (0662) 641331
Fax (0662) 641576
Location in park at foot of Gaisberg, east of city; garages
Meals breakfast, lunch, dinner, snacks
Prices rooms AS1200-3600 with breakfast; meals from AS300
Rooms 12 double, 12 single, 4 suites; all have bath or shower, central heating, phone, TV, safe; some hairdriers, 2 rooms with air conditioning
Facilities dining-room, summer house, terrace; gymnasium, sauna, swimming-pool, conference room
Credit Cards AE, DC, MC, V
Children welcome
Disabled not suitable
Pets accepted **Closed** Nov to just before Easter
Languages English, French, Italian, Spanish
Proprietors Asamer family

Salzburgerland

Castle hotel, Salzburg

Hotel Schloss Mönchstein

We half-expected to see Rapunzel leaning out of the 14thC tower of this imposing and well-known hotel, built on a crag above Salzburg. Instead, we found guests in shorts and open-neck shirts ordering coffee and cake on the terrace. Inside, highly-polished tables and gold plush sofas are reflected in large, gilt mirrors. It all looks very stiff and formal, yet the uniformed staff are young and friendly. Two contrasting dining-rooms offer food for the international clientele: one is named for the Empress Maria Theresa, whose portrait stares down at the green satin chairs and pale apricot linen; next door, the Paris-Lodron is all dark wood and burgundy walls.

Bedrooms are plush without being over-decorated. Number 32, high up under the eaves, is decorated in garden greens; number 11 has a tapestry on the wall. Others, too, have antiques but all have modern bathrooms. Half look over the city, the other half over the gardens. Used by businessmen and touring North Americans and Japanese, it also has guests who settle in for a week at a time. Weddings take place in the small chapel and there are weekend harp concerts.

Nearby Casino; city of Salzburg, reached by Mönchsberg-Lift.

5020 Salzburg, Mönchsberg Park 26
Tel (0662) 8485550
Fax (0662) 848559
Location in large park overlooking Salzburg; car parking outside and in garage
Meals breakfast, lunch, dinner, snacks
Prices rooms AS2000-6500 with breakfast; meals from AS350
Rooms 17 double; all have bath or shower, central heating, phone, TV, minibar, hairdrier, safe **Facilities** 2 dining-rooms, sitting-rooms, bar, terraces, tennis courts
Credit Cards AE, DC, MC, V
Children welcome though not really child-oriented
Disabled access to restaurant and bedrooms with lift/elevator **Pets** accepted; not in restaurants **Closed** never
Languages English, French, Italian, some Japanese
Manager Hubert Hirz

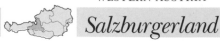

Salzburgerland

City hotel, Salzburg

Hotel Stadtkrug

Even on a chill, rainy afternoon, the Stadtkrug made a favourable impression on our inspector. The manageress greeted him, answered the telephone and welcomed a returning guest, all at the same time and without appearing flustered. That typifies the character of this hotel, which has not been overwhelmed by the year-round influx of tourists. Set in the 800-year old 'new town', it was completely renovated in 1990. Now the ancient beams are exposed above the bar, the stone arches set off white walls and a lump of granite protrudes behind reception, showing where the hotel is built into the Kapuzinerberg.

Most of the bedrooms have the same deep pink carpet, printed curtains, and no-nonsense furnishings, but room 102 boasts a four poster bed. Its bathroom looks straight out of Hollywood but even ordinary bathrooms have two wash-basins and large, well-lit mirrors. Room numbers are hand-painted, in similar style to the Papageno on the elevator doors. The restaurant is one of the most popular in town, staying open late during the Festival. In fine weather, the 4 terrace gardens offer views of church domes and spires.

Nearby Festspielhaus; Dom; Mozarteum; Mirabellgarten.

5020 Salzburg, Linzergasse 20
Tel (0662) 873545
Fax (0662) 879588
Location in pedestrian zone in old town; parking with hotel ticket or in public car park 2 minutes away
Meals breakfast, lunch, dinner, snacks
Prices rooms AS900-3100 with breakfast; meals from AS180
Rooms 31 double, 2 single; all have bath or shower, central heating, phone, TV, radio; some minibars
Facilities 2 dining rooms, 3 sitting rooms, bar, 4 terraces,
Credit Cards AE, DC, MC, V
Children welcome
Disabled not suitable
Pets accepted
Closed 15 Feb to end-March; restaurant only, Tues except during Festival
Languages English, French, Italian
Proprietors Lucian family

Salzburgerland

Suburban villa, Salzburg

Villa Pace

Every great city needs a special, secret hideaway. This is it. Set in the quiet residential area at the foot of the Gaisberg, the Villa Pace (formerly Haus Ingeborg) is a small luxury hotel that attracts actors, conductors, and other celebrities who relish the seclusion. The view is worthy of a tourist board poster: across meadows and trees to the castle, towers, and spires of Salzburg. The 400-year old villa has old beams and hand-woven carpets, rough walls and polished antiques.

A small kitchen with two lady chefs provides a short menu of 'new regional dishes' served in the tiny pearl-grey and pink 'La Pace' restaurant. The hotel is a reflection of the family: the carved heads in the bar and wood panels in the Salon came from a cinema and mill, both family businesses. Upstairs, every bed-room is an harmonious mixture of old and new. A four-poster bed has a wooden canopy and lacy bedspread; a well-known singer always takes the room with a grand piano. The Ober-rauch's have thought of everything: there is a small, heated swimming-pool, sauna and solarium ... even Riedel glasses in the minibars.

Nearby Gaisberg, Kapuzinerberg; Salzburg.

5020 Salzburg,
Sonnleitenweg 9
Tel (0662) 641501
Fax (0662) 64150122
Location in residential area, overlooking Salzburg; covered car parking
Meals breakfast, lunch, dinner, snacks
Prices rooms AS1800-4100 with breakfast; meals from AS400
Rooms 6 double, 2 single, 5 suites; all have bath and shower, central heating, phone, TV, minibar, hairdrier, safe **Facilities** dining-room, sitting-room, terrace; swimming-pool, sauna; free limousine service
Credit Cards AE, DC, MC, V; 3% discount for cash, cheques
Children not suitable
Disabled not suitable
Pets accepted
Closed Nov 1 to March 1
Languages English
Proprietors Oberrauch family

Salzburgerland

Old post inn, St. Gilgen

Gasthof Zur Post

Most visitors to this popular resort on the Wolfgangsee are interested in its Mozart connection. The composer's mother was born in the village and his sister lived here. Even the main square is called Mozartplatz and honours the famous man with a fountain and statue. Our inspector is an architecture buff, however, so he was more interested in the centuries-old town hall and this inn. The Gasthof Zur Post was built in 1415 and is a 'protected' building. One look at the outside explains why: all along the front is a lively painted frieze depicting a medieval boar hunt. Beneath is a neat pile of logs, ready for cold weather.

Inside, the oak beams and dark stone floors continue the ancient ambience. Upstairs, doors boast peasant-style floral patterns. Bedrooms are varied in shape and size, with modern beds and muted colours against cream walls. Views are on to the street or, higher up, rooftops. A few, right on the topmost floor, have a view of the lake. Heinz Müller became the owner in 1991 and, we understand, renovations are planned. While there is room for improvement, we hope changes are made sympathetically. It would be a shame if the historic nature were spoiled.

Nearby Mozart's mother's house, Zwölferhorn cable-car.

5340 St Gilgen, Mozartplatz 8
Tel (06227) 7509
Fax (06227) 698
Location in middle of village, opposite town hall; own car parking
Meals breakfast, lunch, dinner, snacks
Prices rooms AS450-1360 with breakfast; DB&B from AS580; reductions for children; meals from AS150
Rooms 15 double, 5 single, 2 suites; all have bath or shower, central heating, phone, TV
Facilities 3 dining-rooms, bar; terrace; indoor swimming-pool, sauna
Credit Cards not accepted
Children welcome
Disabled not suitable
Pets accepted
Closed Nov
Languages English, French
Proprietors Müller family

Salzburgerland

❊ **Chalet hotel, Wald im Oberpinzgau** ❊

Hotel Schöneben

Our inspectors did not find anywhere better than Stefan Schneider's former farm house at the western end of the Salzach valley. Imagine a perfect Austrian country inn, complete with sloping roof, blue shutters and wooden balconies, weighed down with geraniums. Switch to winter, with snow blanketing the mountains and scuttle inside where the rough, honey-coloured wood lines the thick walls and low ceilings, and crackling open fires bring a glow of pleasure. Stefan comes from Kassel in Germany and wanted it to be "like my own house". The old china plates, rows of books, vases of dried flowers are all in the right places; the floral curtains and pink table-cloths are just the right colours. Words like 'snug', 'cozy' and even '*gemütlich*' really are apt.

The same applies to the bedrooms in the older building. Despite being small, almost cramped, they are aptly-furnished in country style, with balconies. Herr Schneider cleverly expanded the hotel by building suites under the broad terrace. The style is 'modern rustic' and guests are encouraged to bring their own CDs and cassettes to play on the music centres.

Nearby National Park; Krimml Waterfall; winter sports; hiking.

5742 Wald im Pinzgau
Tel (06565) 82890
Fax (06565) 8419
Location above valley road, outside village; car parking outside
Meals breakfast, lunch, dinner, snacks
Prices rooms AS510-1600 with breakfast; reductions for children; meals from AS150
Rooms 12 double, 3 single, 9 suite; all have bath or shower, central heating, phone, radio; TV on request; some minibar
Facilities 3 dining-rooms, TV in *Stube*, games-room; terrace, sauna
Credit Cards not accepted
Children very welcome
Disabled not suitable
Pets not accepted
Closed Nov to mid-Dec; after Easter to mid-May
Languages some English, French
Proprietor Stefan Schneider

Salzburgerland

Gasthof Lebzelter

'Restaurant with rooms' does scant justice to this converted guest-house set among the medieval houses of Werfen. The Obauer brothers were voted 'chefs of the year' in 1989 and reservations must be made well in advance. After several years working abroad, Rudolf and Karl came home to take on the family business that stretches back 150 years. Signature dishes include a trout strudel with white wine sauce, calves' liver with truffles and chestnuts, and sumptuous desserts like blackberry and chocolate parfait, all with the light inventiveness of contemporary French chefs. The decoration is as sophisticated as the food. The two small dining rooms retain the old, low, beamed ceilings, but tables are set formally with fine linen and fresh flowers.

This contemporary feel continues upstairs where, in 1989, an architect friend designed dramatic, geometric headboards for the grey and white minimalist bedrooms. The white bathrooms are as antiseptic as the Obauers' kitchens. For breakfast, *brioches* and home-made breads are served to order, perhaps in the garden under gold and white umbrellas.

Nearby Schloss Hohenwerfen; the Eisriesenwelt ice caves; mountaineering; skiing; Salzburg (30 minutes away).

5450 Werfen, Hauptstr 46
Tel (06468) 2120
Fax (06468) 21212
Location on main street of village; car parking on street
Meals breakfast, lunch, dinner; snacks in café
Prices rooms AS380-650 with breakfast, DB&B AS900-1100; meals from AS275
Rooms 6 double, 1 single; all have bath or shower, central heating, phone, TV, minibar, hairdrier

Facilities 2 dining rooms, terrace
Credit Cards AE
Children not suitable
Disabled not suitable
Pets accepted
Closed variable, always phone ahead
Languages English, French
Proprietors Rudolf and Karl Obauer

Salzburgerland

❋   **Country inn, Zell am See/Thumersbach**   ❋

Landhotel Erlhof

Hans Brudermann is one of Austria's top chefs and is confident enough to allow food to be the focal point of this old farmhouse set on the sunny, quiet side of the Zeller Lake. The clue to Brudermann's philosophy is stencilled on the wall beside the stone-arched entrance: *Essen und Trinken,* eat and drink. "I don't like to call this a restaurant. It's more of a place for people who like to sit and talk, to celebrate, to enjoy an evening out," he says. They do so in the snug dining-room with an open fire under the centuries-old, arched ceiling. Brudermann uses local lake fish and game, goats' cheeses and his own herbs. Venison is wind-dried in a mountain-hut; home-made ravioli is stuffed with black pudding; and raspberries are made into sorbets.

As well as eating and drinking, guests chat in the wood-panelled sitting room, admire the view across the lake to the snow-frosted peaks of the Hohe Tauern, and sleep in plain, straightforward bedrooms.

Some may work off calories with golf, tennis, cycling or swimming from the Erlhof's own beach. When the lake is frozen, some diners even walk across from Zell.

Nearby Zeller Lake; mountains; winter sports.

5700 Zell am See/
Thumersbach, Erlhofweg 11
Tel (06542) 66370
Fax (06542) 663763
Location in own grounds by lake; car parking outside hotel
Meals breakfast, lunch, dinner, snacks
Prices rooms AS550-2000 with breakfast; DB&B from AS700; meals from AS250
Rooms 19 double; all have bath or shower, central heating, phone, TV

Facilities 2 dining-rooms, sitting-room, bar, terrace; sauna, solarium, fitness room, small conference facilities, garden
Credit Cards MC, V
Children accepted
Disabled not suitable
Pets accepted **Closed** Nov to mid-Dec; restaurant only, Tues, Wed lunch
Languages English, French, Italian **Proprietors** Hans and Karin Brudermann

Salzburgerland

 Castle hotel, Zell am See

Schloss Prielau

Anyone familiar with the relative hustle-and-bustle of Zell am See would be surprised to find such a secluded retreat only minutes away. The castle has stood at the northern end of the Zeller lake for 400 years, but it took a major rescue in 1987 to prevent total dilapidation. Now a hotel, Schloss Prielau combines all the latest plumbing and electrical wizardry with a sense of the past. Paintings and carvings by local artists and craftsmen have been restored, and Persian carpets give warmth to tile and wood floors. Rustic chests stand beside solid, comfortable armchairs and sofas.

"Stylish informality" was the reaction of one guest. Manager Helmut Marx, a veteran of the international hotel business, relishes the intimacy of this small castle that takes only 24 guests. Bedrooms are large, with curtains and chairs providing colour against white walls. Every window has a pretty view. Weekenders come from Munich, businessmen for seminars during the week, and families for skiing in winter and golf in summer. There is a private beach, while the *Prielaukirche,* a tiny chapel, is still used for services, weddings and baptisms.

Nearby Skiing in Zell, Kaprun; lake, water-sports; golf.

5700 Zell am See
Tel (06542) 2609
Fax (06542) 260955
Location north end of Zeller lake, in own park; ample car parking
Meals breakfast, dinner
Prices rooms AS950-3000 with breakfast; reductions for children; meals from AS300
Rooms 8 double, 4 single, 1 apartment; all have bath or shower, central heating, phone, TV, minibar

Facilities 2 dining-rooms, sitting-room with bar; terrace, beach; sauna
Credit Cards not accepted
Children welcome
Disabled not suitable
Pets accepted
Closed mid-Oct to mid-Dec; 3 weeks after Easter
Languages English, French, Spanish
Manager Helmut Marx

Salzburgerland

❊   Chalet hotel, Abtenau   ❊

Hotel Lindenhof

The Innermair family value the simple things in life, like high-quality cooking and comfort. Magnificent views of the Tennengebirge mountains. Winter sports include sleigh rides. Indoor health spa; outdoor swimming-pool. Abtenau's ski-lifts 3 km.

■ 5441 Abtenau, Lindenthal 67 **Tel** (06243) 3394 **Fax** (06243) 339416 **Meals** breakfast, lunch, dinner, snacks **Prices** rooms AS350-1100 with breakfast; meals from AS100 **Rooms** 15, all with bath or shower, central heating, phone, **Credit cards** AE, MC, V **Closed** Nov to mid-Dec; after Easter **Languages** English

---

❊   Town hotel, Badgastein   ❊

Hotel Der Lindenhof

In a sunny spot in the middle of this sophisticated resort, the Lindenhof has been in the same family for generations. The restaurant has a deserved reputation; although bedrooms are somewhat plain, they have big windows and balconies.

■ 5640 Badgastein, Poserstr 2 **Tel** (06434) 2614 **Fax** (06434) 261413 **Meals** breakfast, lunch, dinner, snacks **Prices** rooms AS500-1600 with breakfast **Rooms** 22, all with bath or shower, central heating, phone, TV, radio **Credit cards** AE, DC, MC, V **Closed** never **Languages** English, Italian

---

❊   Country hotel, Dorfgastein   ❊

Unterbergerwirt

A real, red fire engine to play on, child-friendly steps and basement washing machine, plus an excellent restaurant, keep the whole family happy. Set in meadows looking across to the Fulseck/Kreuzkogel ski slopes of the Gastein valley.

■ 5632 Dorfgastein, Unterberg 7 **Tel** (06433) 3590 **Fax** (06433) 35959 **Meals** breakfast, lunch, dinner, snacks **Prices** rooms AS360-1000 with breakfast; meals from AS150 **Rooms** 7, all with bath or shower, central heating, phone, TV, radio **Credit cards** not accepted **Closed** mid-Oct to early Dec; after Easter to early May **Languages** English

---

Restaurant with rooms, Fuschl am See

Zur Sägemühle

Franz Nussbaumer decided to convert the family sawmill into a restaurant in 1976. His wife's warm welcome and good cooking make up for the roadside location. Reserve a bedroom at the back, overlooking the stream.

■ 5330 Fuschl am See 16 **Tel** (06226) 416 **Meals** breakfast, lunch, dinner, snacks **Prices** rooms AS680-760 with breakfast (doubles only); meals AS150 **Rooms** 11, all with bath or shower, central heating, phone, radio; TV by request **Credit cards** AD, DC, MC, V **Closed** Nov to late March **Languages** English, Italian

Salzburgerland

✻ Country inn, Goldegg ✻

Hotel Gasthof zur Post

Set in a pretty, unspoilt village with an old castle and church. Views are over the small lake. Winter sports plus golf, hiking, swimming, and fishing in summer. Hearty appetites appreciate the cooking, well above average, using fresh local produce.
■ 5622 Goldegg **Tel** (06415) 81030 **Fax** (06415) 810359 **Meals** breakfast, lunch, dinner, snacks **Prices** rooms DB&B AS575-1800 **Rooms** 30, all with bath or shower, central heating, phone, TV on request **Credit cards** AE, DC, MC, V **Closed** Nov to mid-Dec; after Easter to early May **Languages** English, French, Italian

---

✻ Restaurant with rooms, Hallein ✻

Gasthof Hohlwegwirt

The Kronreif family are well-known for their ambitious restaurant with its imaginative sauces and regional dishes. Although recently renovated, this traditional Wirtshaus retains its 200 year-old atmosphere. Salzburg 20 minutes away; skiing at Zinkenkogel.
■ 5400 Hallein-Taxach, Salzachtal Bundesstr-Nord 62 **Tel** (06245) 824150 **Fax** (06245) 24150 **Meals** breakfast, lunch, dinner, snacks **Prices** rooms AS600-1800 with breakfast **Rooms** 5, all with bath or shower, central heating, phone, TV **Credit cards** not accepted **Closed** never; restaurant only, Mon except during Festival **Languages** English

---

✻ Resort-village hotel, Kaprun ✻

Hotel Kaprunerhof

Just 2 minutes from the middle of Kaprun, this is a quiet hotel. The Schieferer family like to go walking, cycling and golfing with guests, who receive a discount on green fees. 27 holes of golf in the area.
■ 5710 Kaprun **Tel** (06547) 7234 **Fax** (06547) 8581 **Meals** breakfast, lunch, dinner, snacks **Prices** rooms AS590-1450 with breakfast; meals from AS120 **Rooms** 23, all with bath or shower, central heating, phone, TV **Credit cards** MC, V **Closed** never **Languages** English

---

✻ Ancient inn, Leogang ✻

Hotel Kirchenwirt

A fine example of preservation and renovation. The Unterrainer family has been here 100 years; the building dates from 1326. From the carved wooden beds to the panelled restaurant, it all smacks of history and impeccable taste. Excellent food.
■ 5771 Leogang **Tel** (06583) 216 **Fax** (06583) 459 **Meals** breakfast, lunch, dinner, snacks **Prices** rooms AS400-900 with breakfast **Rooms** 23, all with bath or shower, central heating, phone; TV on request **Credit cards** not accepted **Closed** Nov; June **Languages** English

Salzburgerland

❊   Chalet hotel, Mittersill   ❊

Hotel Wieser

Everyone's idea of a country hotel, with the Pinzgauer mountains beyond the meadows. Pale blue curtains and sofas brighten the reception area. Wood-panelling covers walls and ceilings. Family-oriented. Skiing at Kitzbühel-Pass Thurn, 15 minutes.

■ 5730 Mittersill **Tel** (06562) 4270 **Fax** (06562) 427056 **Meals** breakfast, lunch, dinner, snacks **Prices** rooms AS320-700 with breakfast; meals from AS100 **Rooms** 29, all with bath or shower, central heating, phone **Credit cards** not accepted **Closed** Nov to mid-Dec; 1 week after Easter **Languages** English

---

Manor house hotel, Oberalm bei Hallein

Schloss Haunsperg

Filled with antiques and heirlooms, this 600-year old manor house is almost a museum but to the von Gernerth family it is home. Among the portraits of ancestors is great-grandfather, who wrote the words to "The Blue Danube Waltz".

■ 5411 Oberalm/Hallein, Oberalm 32 **Tel** (06245) 2662 **Fax** (06245) 5680 **Meals** breakfast **Prices** rooms AS1350-2460 with breakfast **Rooms** 8, all with bath or shower, phone **Credit cards** AE,DC,MC,V **Closed** never **Languages** English, some French, Italian

---

Mountain inn, Salzburg

Hotel Zistelalm

The look of a hunting-lodge or mountain hut with heavy beams and walls covered in antlers makes quite a contrast to the city down below. This hideaway, high on the Gaisberg, is especially romantic in winter, with its log fires and deep arm-chairs.

■ 5020 Salzburg, Gaisberg **Tel** (0662) 641067 **Fax** (0662) 642618 **Meals** breakfast, lunch, dinner, snacks **Prices** rooms AS275-1000 with breakfast; meals from AS200 **Rooms** 24, all with bath or shower, central heating, phone, TV **Credit cards** AE, DC, MC, V **Closed** mid-Oct to mid-Dec **Languages** English

---

Restaurant with rooms, Strasswalchen

Zum Lebzelter

The main attraction in this town is Greti Gugg's restaurant, highly-rated for traditional dishes like stews, roasts and dumplings. Useful as an overnight stop rather than for a holiday but half-board in the plain bedrooms is good value.

■ 5204 Strasswalchen, Marktplatz 1 **Tel** (06215) 206 **Fax** (06215) 2064 **Meals** breakfast, lunch, dinner, snacks **Prices** rooms AS450-1450 with breakfast; meals from AS200; DB&B AS520 **Rooms** 12, all with bath or shower, central heating, phone, TV **Credit cards** AE, DC, MC, V **Closed** never; restaurant only, Sun evening, Mon **Languages** English

Salzburgerland

❊   Resort hotel, Wagrain   ❊

Hotel Alpina

The emphasis is on sport in this comfortable, well-integrated mixture of old and new. Outsiders visit the restaurant where food is 'light traditional'. Guests can ski from the door to explore the Wagrain-Flachau slopes. Ski-school and kindergarten next door.
■ 5602 Wagrain, Hofmarkt 108 **Tel** (06413) 8337 **Fax** (06413) 833750 **Meals** breakfast, lunch, dinner, snacks **Prices** rooms AS300-1500 with breakfast **Rooms** 20, all with bath or shower, central heating, phone, TV, radio **Credit cards** not accepted **Closed** Oct to early Dec; after Easter to late May **Languages** English, French, Italian

---

❊   Village inn, Wagrain   ❊

Gasthof Grafenwirt

In the middle of this classic, flowery mountain village is the Schindlmaissers' white-painted hotel where folk ornaments brighten plain, modern rooms. Menus change daily; local lamb is a speciality. Good base for exploring Enns Valley.
■ 5602 Wagrain, Markt 14 **Tel** (06413) 8230 **Fax** (06413) 7162 **Meals** breakfast, lunch, dinner **Prices** rooms AS330-680 with breakfast; meals AS120-300 **Rooms** 17 all with bath or shower, phone; some have TV, hairdrier, safe **Credit Cards** not accepted **Closed** Tues (Apr-Oct), last 2 weeks Jun, Oct 20-early Dec depending on snow **Languages** English

---

❊   Twin hotels, Wald im Oberpinzgau   ❊

Hotels Walderwirt and Märzenhof

The Strasser family combine two inns: the 15thC Walderwirt, with wood-panelled dining rooms and intimate fireside seats, is linked by underground passage to the 20thC Märzenhof with its big, glassed-in swimming-pool and modern bedrooms.
■ 5742 Wald im Oberpinzgau 6 **Tel** (06565) 82160 **Fax** (06565) 821614 **Meals** breakfast, lunch, dinner, snacks **Prices** rooms AS490-1580 with breakfast **Rooms** 20, all with bath or shower, central heating, phone, TV, radio **Credit cards** MC, V **Closed** Nov to mid-Dec; mid-April to mid-May **Languages** English, French, Italian

---

❊   Chalet hotel, Zell am See   ❊

Hotel 'Der Metzgerwirt'

The old building, with dark timbers punctuated by small windows and green shutters, celebrates its 500th birthday in 1993. Brand-new in 1990, but using old wood inside, is the annexe behind, built round a courtyard, complete with rose-garden.
■ 5700 Zell am See, Saalfeldnerstr 5 **Tel** (06542) 25200 **Fax** (06542) 252034 **Meals** breakfast, lunch, dinner, snacks **Prices** rooms AS450-2000 with breakfast; meals from AS110 **Rooms** 31, all with bath or shower, central heating, phone, TV **Credit cards** DC **Closed** never **Languages** English

Oberösterreich

Hotels in Upper Austria

Upper Austria boasts a variety of landscape, including mountains like the Höllengebirge and the northern slopes of the Totes Gebirge; the broad valley of the Danube; a large part of the Salzkammergut and its lakes. Towns like Linz, the state capital, gave us the renowned *Linzertorte* cake while *Palatschinken*, Upper Austria's pancakes, are now regarded as a national dish.

Aigen im Mühlkreis is an attractive old town in the Mühlviertel near the Czech border, where Christine Wöber's modern Hotel Waldhof Axberg enjoys a fine reputation (Tel (07281) 8585, 54 rooms). Peter Gruber's Sporthotel Almesberger on the old market square may be more to the visitors' taste as it is old-fashioned (Tel (07281) 87130, fax 871376, 57 rooms). West of Freistadt in Bad Leonfelden is the Böhmertor, open year-round and particularly good for families with small children (Tel (07213) 429, 28 rooms). In Neufelden, Albert and Barbara Sammer's Gasthof Sammer with its pink façade, geraniums and arches overlooking the market-square has many fans (Tel (07282) 233, fax 2236, 17 rooms). The same goes for Erika Raab's Hotel Weinberg in Rutzenmoos (Tel (07672) 3302, fax 330238, 23 rooms) as it is handy for the Linz-Salzburg motorway, near Vöcklabruck.

On the German border, the old town of Braunau on the Inn River still has photogenic old houses and two old inns for an overnight stay. The more comfortable is the Schüdlbauer (Tel (07722) 7339, 7 rooms); somewhat simpler is the Alter Weinhans (Tel (07722) 3396, 5 rooms). Look out for the Hotel Mader in Katsdorf (Tel (07235) 8585, 26 rooms) and let us know what you think of this bustling hotel by following the instructions on page 192.

Down on the Mondsee, the famous Weisses Kreuz restaurant had 10 bedrooms, but Gustav Lugerbauer told our inspector that he was converting them into self-catering apartments. (Tel (06232) 2254, 10 rooms).

Steyr is one of Austria's loveliest old towns, straddling the Enns and Steyr rivers. There are two attractive but large hotels to stay in here. The Hotel Mader on the main square is well known for its food as well as its comfort (Tel (07252) 533580, fax 533506, 60 rooms). The Romantik Hotel Minichmayr is equally attractive (Tel (07252) 53410, fax 4820255, 50 rooms).

For further details about the area, contact:
Landesverband für Tourismus in Oberösterreich,
Schillerstrasse 50,
A-4010 Linz
Tel: (0732) 663021
Fax: (0732) 600220

This page acts as an introduction to the features and hotels of Oberösterreich and gives brief recommendations of good hotels that for one reason or another have not made a full entry. The long entries for this state – covering the hotels we are most enthusiastic about – start on the next page. But do not neglect the shorter entries starting on page 99: these are all hotels that we would happily stay at.

Oberösterreich

Lakeside hotel, Attersee

Gasthof Häupl

This is a winning combination: cooking by a top chef and views across the largest lake in the Austrian Alps. Early booking, therefore, is essential, particularly on sunny summer weekends. Even in winter, gourmets phone ahead for a table in one of the two *Stüberl*. They come for regional specialities like fish from the lake or dumplings stuffed with bacon, accompanied by one of half a dozen wines available daily by the glass, or beer from the barrel.

There has been an inn here for over 300 years. The Häupl family have run it for a mere seven generations during which they have collected some eye-catching antiques. A confessional, complete with a statue of St. Florian on top, is a telephone booth; nearby is an ancient wine press. Small alcoves with tables and chairs are cosy spots for reading or chatting. As for bedrooms, number 121 is particularly striking with its black and white *Wiener Werkstätte* (Vienna Workshop) furniture and a print of a Gustav Klimt landscape on the wall. Others are simpler, but bathrooms are slick and new, with grey or white tiles and power showers. All this, and breakfast on the terrace overlooking the Attersee.

Nearby Attersee's churches; water-sports; para-gliding.

4863 Seewalchen am Attersee, Hauptstr 20-22
Tel (07662) 2249
Fax (07662) 882262
Location above village on edge of lake; car parking outside
Meals breakfast, lunch, dinner, snacks
Prices AS875-2850 with breakfast; reductions for children; meals from AS300
Rooms 25 double, 10 single; all have bath or shower, central heating, phone, TV, minibar; some have hairdrier
Facilities 3 dining-rooms, breakfast-room, bar; terrace, sauna
Credit Cards AE, DC, MC, V
Children not accepted
Disabled access to 3 rooms
Pets accepted
Closed never
Languages English, French, Italian
Proprietors Häupl family

Oberösterreich

Lakeside hotel, Attersee

Gasthof Föttinger

'Do what Gustav Mahler did' is the motto of this 19thC hotel which capitalizes on the 'Mahler connection'. Inside the large, open-plan lobby is a display case of Mahler memorabilia including some songs, a small bust of the great man and a copy of his 3rd Symphony. He wrote this, along with the 2nd Symphony, in a small summer cabin he put up by the lake. That was back in 1893-96 and he was visited by his friend, the conductor Bruno Walter, who arrived by steamer. These boats still ferry people around the lake and the garden is still used for concerts and musical evenings. The flowery meadows which were there in the composer's day are now covered by caravans.

That is the drawback to staying here. The hotel is right on the lake but views from the green-shuttered windows are blotted by a caravan park at its busiest in July and August. Otherwise, the bedrooms are all generously-sized, with white walls and modern pine furniture: 'functional' to some, 'anonymous' to others. The restaurant is similarly expansive, with a rustic look thanks to antlers and the brown colour scheme. Meat is a speciality, since the butcher's shop has been part of the hotel since 1912.

Nearby Salzkammergut; Höllengebirge; Neukirchen Game Park.

4853 Steinbach am Attersee, Seefeld 14
Tel (07663) 342
Fax (07663) 34242
Location on edge of lake; own car parking area
Meals breakfast, lunch, dinner, snacks
Prices AS370-500 with breakfast; DB&B from AS600; reductions for children; meals from AS200
Rooms 21 double, 5 single, 2 suites; all have bath or shower, central heating, phone, TV, hairdrier, radio
Facilities 3 dining-rooms, bar; terrace, garden, private beach; indoor swimming-pool
Credit Cards MC
Children very welcome
Disabled not suitable
Pets tolerated
Closed Dec
Languages English, French
Proprietors Föttinger family

Oberösterreich

Lakeside villa, Attersee

Villa Langer

With porches and balconies, gables and bay windows, this is a classic 'summer resort' villa from the turn of the century. Except for the vine that now covers one wall, it cannot have changed much over the years. Our inspector was happy to settle himself on a Biedermeier sofa and read the newspaper, then take a late coffee in the sunny white conservatory.

The villa is at the south-east corner of the Attersee. Behind, a rocky, wooded cliff veers up steeply; in front is the water. Unfortunately, between house and shore is the road that circumnavigates the lake. Guests must cross it to reach the private boathouse with garden and windsurfers for hire.

Dinner may be booked five nights a week for those not wanting to cook. Each of the 13 suites has a kitchenette and some have two bathrooms, making them suitable for large families. Furnishings are a mixture of 19thC and modern; some rooms have original neo-Gothic painted ceilings; most have views of the lake. None have televisions. This is an informal, peaceful place in the Salzkammergut 'for those who can amuse themselves and don't need attractions'. Pets are welcome, 'but no snakes or lions'.

Nearby lake, resorts; Weissbacher Sattl; Weissenbach gorge.

4854 Weissenbach, Attersee
Tel (07663) 242
Fax (07663) 24236
Location on lake-side road at foot of Höllen mountains; own car parking area
Meals breakfast
Prices rooms AS530-1060 with breakfast; reduction for children
Rooms 4 double, 2 single, 13 apartments with kitchenettes; all have bath or shower, central heating, phone, radio, minibar, hairdrier
Facilities 2 dining-rooms, breakfast room, sitting-room, bar; terrace; sauna
Credit Cards not accepted
Children very welcome
Disabled not suitable
Pets accepted
Closed early Dec
Languages English, French, Italian
Manageress Petra Steiner

Oberösterreich

Castle hotel, Bad Hall

Schloss Feyregg

This is a 'dream *Schloss*', as full of atmosphere as it is of history. Mentioned in an 11thC chronicle, it actually goes back even further, to the 8thC. The castle seen today, however, dates from 1720. The seclusion is total; as for silence, 'a cemetery would be noisier', according to our inspector. He delighted in the gardens: from the long avenue lined with statues, to the inner courtyard and wilder garden beyond. The mixture of furnishings from different ages is a happy one.

The high ceilings have a medieval look, while elaborate baroque doors lead to the breakfast room, where paintings of 19thC society ladies adorn the walls. Each of the bedrooms has its own little sitting-room with, perhaps, a 19thC *chaise longue,* a writing desk, or prints of the Hapsburg military on the walls. This is the furniture that was in the castle when Frau Harmer's family bought it in 1937, so it still looks and feels like a private house. Josie the dachshund welcomes visitors and other small dogs. Views are over the gardens or of the church in the sleepy little town of Bad Hall. Just below the castle is an old inn where guests often have lunch or dinner.

Nearby fishing, golf; mineral springs.

4540 Bad Hall
Tel (07258) 2594
Location just outside Bad Hall; own car parking
Meals breakfast
Prices rooms AS850-1700 with breakfast
Rooms 4 double, 2 single in castle, 3 single in garden annexe, 2 suites; all have bath or shower, central heating
Facilities breakfast-room, billiard room
Credit Cards not accepted

Children accepted if well behaved
Disabled not suitable
Pets accepted
Closed Christmas
Languages some English, French
Proprietor Ruth Maria Harmer

Oberösterreich

Town hotel, Freistadt

Gasthof Zum Goldenen Hirschen

Freistadt has managed to conserve much of its medieval heritage. The ancient moat is green with grass but the doorways, balconies and windows tell a story that is hundreds of years old. The town even has a nightwatchman. This guest-house is just inside the square Bohemian Gate and the garden backs onto the old walls. Built after the great fires of the early 1500s, it was rebuilt and given a new façade some 100 years ago.

Our inspector was delighted by the swallows in the arched passage where old wine presses and a hay cutter lend an aura of rusticity. In the vaulted, Gothic dining hall, the marriage of owners Johann and Anna Kronberger in 1867 is recorded on the ceiling, but it has been in the present family only since 1913. The cooking is imaginative, with traditional dishes matched by, for example, a pumpernickel soufflé with cheese sauce. Bedrooms are large and some have a separate sitting area; the best offer a view across the town towards the Gothic church. Our inspector liked the two pretty *Stüberln,* the terrace at the back, and the cheerful young owners who have recently expanded into the house next door.

Nearby old town of Freistadt; Mühlviertel.

4240 Freistadt, Böhmergasse 8-10
Tel (07942) 22580
Fax (07942) 225840
Location on old city street, near Böhmer Tor; public car-parking
Meals breakfast, lunch, dinner, snacks
Prices rooms AS420-660 with breakfast; DB&B from AS500; reductions for children; meals from AS120
Rooms 16 double, 7 single; all have bath or shower, central heating, phone, TV, radio
Facilities 4 dining-rooms, sitting-room, bar, TV room; terrace
Credit Cards not accepted
Children welcome
Disabled not suitable
Pets accepted
Closed 3 weeks Jan
Languages English, French
Proprietors Deim family

Oberösterreich

Castle hotel, Gmunden

Schlosshotel 'Freisitz Roith'

Most towns would be happy to have one castle; Gmunden has several. The most famous is the 17thC *'Seeschloss';* Freisitz Roith is older by some 100 years. A coat of arms engraved above the entrance boasts of a history dating back to the 16thC. Set in a park of some seven hectares (about 18 acres), it sits grandly on a hill on the eastern shore of Traunsee lake. Herr Prechtl, wearing *Lederhosen* and with a dagger in his sock, showed our inspector round. The entrance is impressive: decorative wrought-iron gates open to the reception area where Renaissance chairs in carved oak look ready for a duke, if not a king.

Do not expect the luxury of some castle hotels. Most bedrooms look over the water but they vary in size and style, and are priced accordingly; more if they have baroque-style beds, a good deal less for those with rather boring modern furniture. A hotel since 1968, it is popular with locals for weddings.

This is the sort of place people either love or hate: take the full-sized, stuffed peacock with outspread tail above the stairway. A novelty or just bizarre? If it is the latter, this is probably not the place for you.

Nearby Gmunden town hall; Schloss Ort; Grünberg cable-car.

4810 Gmunden am Traunsee, Traunsteinstr 87
Tel (07612) 4905
Fax (07612) 490517
Location on hill overlooking Traunsee; car parking in front of hotel
Meals breakfast, lunch, dinner, snacks
Prices AS400-1130 with breakfast; DB&B from AS580; reductions for children; meals from AS180
Rooms 20 double, 7 single, 2 suites; all have bath or shower, central heating, phone, TV, minibar
Facilities 5 dining-rooms, bar; terrace; gymnasium, sauna
Credit Cards AE, MC
Children welcome
Disabled not suitable
Pets accepted
Closed Jan, Feb
Languages English, French, Italian
Proprietors Prechtl family

Oberösterreich

❊ **Mountain inn, Grünau im Almtal** ❊

Romantik Hotel Almtalhof

'This is more of an experience than a hotel. Stand on the balcony on a spring evening and breathe in the fresh, alpine air of the Alm valley. Lilac bloom in the garden below; further on is the rushing river, between birch, chestnut and sycamore trees.' Our inspector continued to enthuse about the 'wonderfully rambling, seemingly endless *Stüberl* and connecting corridors.' Around one corner is a family of straw dolls; everywhere are cushions embroidered in red and white folk designs by Ulrike Leithner, who with her husband, Karl, runs the hotel.

They are gradually improving the 1911 building, built by a Leithner grandfather. Bedrooms, for instance, are being enlarged. Karl made most of their pine furniture, including the carved four-poster bed in Number 11. Bathrooms show similar care and are fitted with power showers and gilded taps. The food is Austrian with a light touch, using produce from local farms and plenty of game. Our inspector was pleased also by the detailed wine list which includes bottles from Austria's finest vineyards. Add an indoor swimming-pool, a garden for children, and a new golf course nearby and you have 'paradise'.

Nearby golf, hiking, cycling; winter sports; Almsee

4645 Grünau im Almtal
Tel (07616) 82040
Fax (07616) 820466
Location valley of River Alm; ample car parking
Meals breakfast, lunch, dinner, snacks
Prices AS560-1600 with breakfast; DB&B AS790; reductions for children; meals from AS230
Rooms 16 double, 3 single, 2 suites; all have bath or shower, central heating, phone, TV, hairdrier, radio, safe
Facilities 2 dining-rooms, café, bar; terrace, health spa; indoor swimming-pool
Credit Cards AE, MC, V
Children very welcome
Disabled 1 bedroom specially adapted
Pets accepted
Closed mid-Oct to mid-Dec; after Easter to end April
Languages English, French
Proprietors Leithner family

Oberösterreich

Bed-and-breakfast hotel, Linz

Wolfinger

There are no undiscovered gems in Linz, where the old quarter attracts tourists from all over the world. Located right on the Hauptplatz is this hotel, whose 19thC façade hides a history dating back hundreds of years, most recently as an inn, before that as a monastery. There is little of the monks' austerity nowadays about the comfortable rooms and tasteful furnishings. Old mirrors, photographs and Biedermeier and art nouveau furniture continue the sense of the old, but bathrooms have the very latest in fittings. Large, white-tiled and with huge mirrors, they have the strong lighting professional make-up artists like but the rest of us find cruel. Most of the bedrooms overlook the quiet, inner courtyard; a few have a view over the square.

The comings and goings on the Hauptplatz can also be seen from the breakfast room, 'if you are lucky enough to get a seat at the window.' Another feature here is the *Bürgertisch,* a table dating from 1889 and inscribed with the names of prominent city councillors. Because the hotel is so busy, our inspector advises double-checking reservations 24 hours before arrival. Cars may be unloaded at the door.

Nearby Pillar of the Holy Trinity, Minorite Church, Mozart Haus.

4020 Linz, Hauptplatz 19
Tel (0732) 7732910
Fax (0732) 77329155
Location on main square of old town; public car park
Meals breakfast
Prices AS950-1200 with breakfast
Rooms 27 double, 3 single; all have bath or shower, central heating, phone, TV, hairdrier
Facilities breakfast-room, sitting-room; terrace
Credit Cards AE, DC, MC, V

Children not accepted
Disabled not suitable
Pets accepted
Closed never
Languages German only
Proprietor Gerhard Dangl

Oberösterreich

Town hotel, Molln

Gasthof Martinsklause

A winding road, with marvellous views of the emerald-green Steyr river, leads to this pretty village and solid, white inn. Facing the church on the main square, the 18thC building has a long garden at the back, with tables for eating under the chestnut trees and loungers for lazing in the sun. Inside, the atmosphere is genuinely welcoming thanks to the congenial owner, Christine Köhler. She is the fourth generation in this family of inn-keepers and the experience shows. This is one of those well-run places where everything happens smoothly, with no visible effort.

One dining-room features stained glass windows, another has beams of ancient oak. Lunchtime is particularly busy, so get there early for the full choice of daily specials. Afterwards, try one of their notable distilled spirits, including several brandies made from blackberries, rowanberries and Wachau grapes. In the public rooms, the colour schemes based on cheerful shades of orange or red are typical of many country inns. Bedrooms have simple, modern furniture and small but practical bathrooms. With a playground and nearby tennis courts, this would be a cost-effective base for families.

Nearby tennis, fishing, hiking.

4591 Molln, am Kirchplatz 129
Tel (07584) 29160
Location on main square of village; car parking outside
Meals breakfast, lunch, dinner, snacks
Prices AS380-760 with breakfast; DB&B from AS495; reductions for children; meals from AS115
Rooms 10 double, 3 single; all have bath or shower, central heating, phone, minibar
Facilities 3 dining-rooms, sitting-room with TV, bar; terrace
Credit Cards not accepted
Children welcome
Disabled not suitable
Pets accepted
Closed 2 weeks in summer; 2 weeks in Jan
Languages English, French
Proprietor Christine Köhler

Oberösterreich

Restaurant with rooms, Mondsee

Landhaus Eschlböck

Reservations are essential if you want to sample some of the best cooking in Austria. Karl Eschlböck is the chef and his 'new Austrian' style works wonders with char and sander. Other dishes range from sole on a bed of asparagus to pot roast of duck with potato soufflé and red cabbage.

Unfortunately, the full effect of the lake-view is lessened by the main road which runs between the hotel and the water. Although traffic has to slow down because of a steep bend, it remains a distraction, particularly for the bedrooms above. For this reason, these are less expensive than the quieter ones at the back. At least a tunnel under the road provides easy access to the private dock and beach. The inn dates back 400 years but this family have been here only since 1952. Karl Eschlböck has been in charge since 1972, and now his reputation attracts businessmen and weekenders as well as Salzburg Festival-goers. Our inspector found the atmosphere rather impersonal, perhaps because the emphasis is on food rather than the hotel. He did notice, however, a lectern with carved eagle which belonged to Herr Eschlböck's great-grandfather, who was Mayor of Vienna.

Nearby Mondsee parish church; Rauchhaus open-air museum.

5310 Mondsee/Plomberg
Tel (06232) 3166
Fax (06232) 316620
Location on lakeside road overlooking lake; ample car parking
Meals breakfast, lunch, dinner
Prices AS500-2500; reductions for children; meals from AS200
Rooms 9 double, 2 single, 1 suite; all have bath or shower, central heating, phone, TV, minibar

Facilities 4 dining-rooms, bar; terrace, sauna, beach on lake
Credit Cards AE, DC, MC, V
Children welcome
Disabled ramp to upper floor
Pets accepted
Closed Jan
Languages English, French, Italian
Proprietor Karl Eschlböck

Oberösterreich

Hotel-restaurant, Mondsee

Leitnerbräu

This scores for location: right in the old part of this attractive town, among pink, blue, and yellow houses and opposite the church of St. Michael with its glorious baroque façade. The lake is only a 10-minute walk away. In fine weather, people like to sit outside under the red and white-striped awning; where better to people-watch?

The wrought-iron sign above, with lions rampant, hop leaves and barrel reflects the brewhouse origins of this restaurant-with-rooms. The host is Olaf Marschallinger, a man who enjoys meeting people, speaks his mind and is ready to put the world to rights. His wife's domain is the kitchen, where she makes traditional Austrian specialities such as *Bauernschmaus,* a mixed meat dish with dumplings. This is not the place for dainty appetites: portions are fulsome and tasty.

Although the 18thC building is listed for its historical interest, the interior was renovated in l990. The occasional Biedermeier chest of drawers, oil painting and stained glass window were retained but the overall look is modern. The atmosphere is genteel; go elsewhere if you want discos.

Nearby Mondsee lake; monastery; local museum.

5310 Mondsee
Tel (06232) 2219
Fax (06232) 221922
Location in middle of village; car parking in own yard
Meals breakfast, lunch, dinner, snacks
Prices rooms AS740-960 for 2 with breakfast; DB&B from AS580; meals from AS150
Rooms 9 double, 1 family; all have bath or shower, central heating, phone, TV; some have hairdrier

Facilities dining-room, breakfast-room; sauna
Credit Cards AC, DC, MC, V
Children welcome
Disabled not suitable
Pets accepted
Closed Nov
Languages English, some Italian
Proprietors Marschallinger family

Oberösterreich

✼ **Waterside hotel, Neufelden** ✼

Mühltalhof

The Rachingers are continuing an inn-keeping tradition going back six generations. The atmosphere in their 17thC hotel is very personal: there are family photographs on the walls, and more in an album near the entrance. Father and daughter run the administrative side, mother and son do the cooking, which is much-praised. Fish and game appear on the ever-changing menu which could include trout mousse with crayfish sauce and venison medallions with redcurrant jelly. Complementing the food is a well-chosen list of wines from France, Italy and Austria, including a personal supply of Styrian wines from a brother-in-law.

Not surprisingly, families enjoy the informality. The playground comes with a children's house, the old mill-pond provides swimming and rowing, and there is a private tennis-court. Over half the rooms look over the water. Those at the top of the building have small windows and wood panelling, creating an effect that could be 'small and cosy' or 'dark and cramped', according to mood and personal taste. Larger bedrooms with balconies are recommended for those with children who need to dry swimwear and towels.

Nearby Danube River; Mühlviertel; tennis; winter sports.

4120 Neufelden
Tel (07282) 2580
Fax (07282) 2583
Location on a minor road, overlooking old mill-pond; ample car parking
Meals breakfast, lunch, dinner, snacks
Prices AS450-800 with breakfast; DB&B from AS600; reductions for children; meals from AS150
Rooms 17 double, 3 single, 6 suites; all have bath or shower, central heating, phone, TV, minibar, hairdrier, safe
Facilities 3 dining-rooms, sitting-room, bar, TV room; terrace; sauna
Credit Cards AE, DC
Children welcome
Disabled not suitable
Pets accepted
Closed Nov
Languages English, French, Italian
Proprietors Rachinger family

Oberösterreich

Town inn, Schärding

Förstingers Wirtshaus

The inspector who visited this town is not given to hyperbole but by the end of the evening, he waxed lyrical: 'turn off the main street, under medieval arches to the bank of the fast-flowing Inn and find your waiter setting out his fishing lines at 10 pm, while swans breast the stream, mallard croak and teal fall out of the darkness and into the water like stones.' Locals boast that their main square is the 'prettiest in Austria' and our man reckoned the claim was justified. The look is pure story-book, with baroque houses painted ochre, red or light blue.

The guest-house dates back to 1606 and its interior continues the atmosphere of days-gone-by, with old beams, vaulted ceilings and intricate carving. Bedrooms have wooden headboards, either genuine antiques or reproductions, with cream walls offsetting the green-painted wood. In the dining-room, formality rules, with pink linens, long-stemmed glasses and candle-light giving a glow to the elaborate pine panelling. The cooking is impressive, with the emphasis on fish, such as carp, *Seibling,* and trout from nearby mountain streams. No doubt fly-fishermen flushed with success can have their catch cooked for dinner.

Nearby city of Schärding; Danube River; Passau.

4780 Schärding am Inn,
Unterer Stadtplatz 3
Tel (07712) 23020
Fax (07712) 23023
Location on main square; own unattended car parking area
Meals breakfast, lunch, dinner, snacks
Prices rooms AS685-1065; reductions for children; meals from AS150
Rooms 14 double, 2 single; all have bath or shower, central heating, phone, TV, minibar,

hairdrier, safe
Facilities dining-room
Credit Cards AE, DC, MC, V
Children welcome
Disabled not suitable
Pets accepted
Closed never
Languages English
Proprietors Förstinger family

Oberösterreich

Lakeside hotel, Attersee

Hotel-Seegasthof Oberndorfer

Right on the Attersee lake, this resort-hotel is well-known for its restaurant which specializes in lake fish. A few pieces of old furniture, but the modern bedrooms have white walls, sparse decoration and quilted bedspreads in pastel shades.

■ 4864 Attersee, Hauptstr 18 **Tel** (07666) 364 **Fax** (07666) 36491 **Meals** breakfast, lunch, dinner, snacks **Prices** rooms AS540-2100 with breakfast; meals from AS100 **Rooms** 28, all with bath or shower, central heating, phone, TV, minibar **Credit cards** not accepted **Closed** Jan, Feb **Languages** English, French, Spanish

---

✤ Country hotel, Attersee at Unterach ✤

Hotel Georgshof

Set in fields above the southern end of the Attersee, the hotel's terraces maximize views of the surrounding woods and fields. Walks and tennis-courts nearby. The dining-room and bedrooms are square and box-like. Indoor swimming pool.

■ 4866 Unterach 320 **Tel** (07665) 8501 **Fax** (07665) 85018 **Meals** breakfast, lunch, dinner, snacks **Prices** rooms AS320-1000 with breakfast; meals from AS100 **Rooms** 25, all with bath or shower, central heating, phone, TV **Credit cards** AE, DC, MC, V **Closed** never **Languages** English

---

Restaurant with rooms, Bad Hall

Hofwirt Gasthof Schröck

Four centuries of hospitality continue, with Johanna Unterreiter-Schröck's cooking drawing guests to Hehenberg on the edge of Bad Hall. Dishes include local fish such as char and carp. Comfortable rooms above. Popular with fly fishermen.

■ 4540 Bad Hall, Hehenberg 1 **Tel** (07258) 2274 **Meals** breakfast, lunch, dinner **Prices** rooms AS300-600 with breakfast; meals AS140 **Rooms** 3, all with bath **Credit Cards** AE **Closed** Mon, Tues; Nov; New Year **Languages** English, French

---

✤ Country guest-house, Bad Leonfelden ✤

Berggasthof Waldschenke am Sternstein

Up a forest road on the edge of the Bohemian woods and near the Czech border, this Alpine house has fresh, pretty bedrooms with floral-patterned curtains. Surprisingly smart dining-room with well-prepared food. The owner's fox-terrier rather aggressive.

■ 4190 Bad Leonfelden **Tel** (07213) 6279 **Meals** breakfast, lunch, dinner, snacks **Prices** rooms AS260-640 with breakfast; meals from AS150 **Rooms** 12, all with bath or shower, central heating **Credit cards** not accepted **Closed** Nov, Dec; 2 weeks in April **Languages** English, French, Czech

Oberösterreich

Restaurant with rooms, Bad Schallerbach

Hotel-restaurant Grünes Türl

With its sunny terrace, this 200-year old tavern is popular with locals and visitors. Doris and Ingrid Ameshofer's cooking is highly-praised, especially regional dishes of trout and venison. Newer bedrooms have bathrooms; the older ones have showers.

■ 4701 Bad Schallerbach, Gebersdorf 1 **Tel** (07249) 8163 **Fax** (07249) 2932 **Meals** breakfast, lunch, dinner, snacks **Prices** rooms AS460-1400 with breakfast; meals from AS110 **Rooms** 30, all with bath or shower, central heating, phone, TV **Credit cards** AE, DC, MC, V **Closed** never **Languages** English

---

Town hotel, Enns

Hotel-Restaurant Lauriacum

In contrast to the attractive 16thC houses and churches nearby, the Lauriacum has modern bedrooms, a country-style *Stüberl* and a secluded garden. Josef Angerer's cooking is outstanding. Used both by businessmen and holiday-makers.

■ 4470 Enns, Wienerstr 5-7 **Tel** (07223) 2315 **Fax** (07223) 233229 **Meals** breakfast, lunch, dinner **Prices** rooms AS650-1050 with breakfast; meals AS150-220 **Rooms** 30, all with bath, TV, phone, minibar **Credit Cards** MC, V **Closed** Sat (restaurant only), Christmas, New Year **Languages** English, French, some Italian

---

Old inn, Freistadt

Gasthof Jäger zum Goldenen Adler

An old inn in an equally old city; part of the medieval walls are built into the hotel. Unusual glassed-in corridors overlook the covered central courtyard. Modern bedrooms are actually more pleasant than the older ones.

■ 4240 Freistadt, Salzgasse 1 **Tel** (07942) 2112 **Fax** (07942) 211244 **Meals** breakfast, lunch, dinner, snacks **Prices** rooms AS380-750 with breakfast; meals from AS90 **Rooms** 30, all with bath or shower, central heating, phone, TV **Credit cards** AE, DC **Closed** 2 weeks Nov **Languages** English, Italian, Czech

---

Lakeside hotel, Gmunden

Waldhotel Marienbrücke

In a peaceful, wooded park, the Obermayr family hotel and restaurant is delightful. Fish, from the lake or sea, are a speciality, cooked with flair. Bedrooms are plain, but were upgraded and modernized recently. Fly-fishing courses available.

■ 4810 Gmunden, An der Marienbrücke 5 **Tel** (07612) 4011 **Fax** (07612) 267954 **Meals** breakfast, lunch, dinner, snacks **Prices** rooms AS430-1300 with breakfast; meals from AS180 **Rooms** 15, all with bath or shower, central heating, phone, TV **Credit cards** AE, DC, MC, V **Closed** early Nov; last 3 weeks Jan **Languages** English

Oberösterreich

❊   Restaurant with rooms, Hellmonsödt   ❊

Gasthof Michelland

Walter Lugmayr and his Swiss wife, Vreni, run the popular Swiss Grill restaurant in the middle of town. Fondues and *flambés* are specialities. Above are plain, practical bedrooms. Children very welcome. Kirchschlag ski area 5 minutes away by car.

■ 4202 Hellmonsödt 11 **Tel** (07215) 22380 **Meals** breakfast, lunch, dinner, snacks **Prices** rooms AS220-600 with breakfast; meals from AS100 **Rooms** 10, most with bath or shower; all with central heating, phone, TV **Credit cards** AE **Closed** never **Languages** English, French

---

❊   Country hotel, Hinterstoder   ❊

Pension Dietlgut

In an unspoilt valley, surrounded by meadows and pine forest, the Wendl family offer bedrooms and self-catering apartments. Fly-fishing and hiking in summer; cross-country trails at the door; 10 minutes' walk to Bärenalm lift for downhill skiing.

■ 4573 Hinterstoder, Hinterstoder 99 **Tel** (07564) 52480 **Fax** (07564) 524839 **Meals** breakfast, lunch, dinner, snacks **Prices** rooms AS400-1000 with breakfast; meals from AS120 **Rooms** 18, all with bath or shower, central heating, phone **Credit cards** AE **Closed** mid-Oct to mid-Dec; 2 weeks April **Languages** English

---

Cliff-top hotel, Hofkirchen

Hotel Falkner

The spectacular setting makes the Falkner family hotel special. Both open and glassed-in terraces have giddy views of the Danube. Contemporary furniture, pastel colours, paintings on the walls, flowers. Excellent touring base for Mühlviertel.

■ 4142 Hofkirchen, Marsbach 2 **Tel** (07285) 223 **Fax** (07285) 22320 **Meals** breakfast, lunch, dinner, snacks **Prices** rooms AS150-900 with breakfast; meals from AS100 **Rooms** 14, all with bath or shower, central heating, phone, TV **Credit cards** not accepted **Closed** Nov to mid-Dec; mid Jan-March **Languages** English

---

City hotel, Linz

Hotel Drei Mohren

The original building may date from 1595, composer Anton Bruckner may have slept here, but this is really a contemporary, central, city hotel with smart, modern bathrooms. The beige and brown suits businessmen who stay here during the week.

■ 4020 Linz, Promenade 17 **Tel** (0732) 772626 **Fax** (0732) 7726266 **Meals** breakfast **Prices** rooms AS450-950 with breakfast **Rooms** 25, all with bath or shower, central heating, phone, TV, minibar **Credit cards** AE, DC, MC, V **Closed** never **Languages** English, French, Italian

Oberösterreich

Restaurants with rooms, Linz

Gasthof Goldener Adler

Near the middle of Linz, this pleasant bed-and-breakfast is a converted private house. With its modernized bedrooms and cheerful breakfast room, this is an ideal base to explore the old city. The Nudeloper restaurant below is popular with locals.

■ 4040 Linz-Urfahr, Hauptstr 56 **Tel** (0732) 231147 **Fax** (0732) 2311475 **Meals** breakfast; meals in restaurants below **Prices** rooms AS350-950 with breakfast; meals from AS150 **Rooms** 26, all with bath or shower, central heating, phone, TV **Credit cards** not accepted **Closed** never **Languages** English, French, Italian

---

Lakeside hotel, Mondsee

Seehotel Lackner

Even locals enjoy the 15-minute stroll from town to the lakeside terrace to eat *Topfenstrudel* while admiring the view of water and mountains. As well as water-sports, golf and tennis are available nearby. Rooms are plain but comfortable.

■ 5310 Mondsee, Gaisberg 33 **Tel** (06232) 2359 **Fax** (06232) 235950 **Meals** breakfast, lunch, dinner, snacks **Prices** rooms AS390-1680 with breakfast; meals from AS150 **Rooms** 17, all with bath or shower, central heating, phone **Credit cards** not accepted **Closed** never **Languages** English, Italian

---

Riverside hotel, Ottensheim

Donauhof

Although the Donauhof is a square, modern block on the banks of the Danube, it is a sophisticated combination of hotel, restaurant and café. Every Thursday, the Landls have a gourmet evening. Rooms are stark, but quiet. 12 km from Linz.

■ 4100 Ottensheim, An der Fähre **Tel** (07234) 3818 **Fax** (07234) 3825 **Meals** breakfast, lunch, dinner, snacks **Prices** rooms AS490-800 with breakfast; meals from AS100 **Rooms** 12, all with bath or shower, central heating, phone, TV **Credit cards** AE, DC **Closed** never **Languages** English

---

Lakeside hotel, St Wolfgang

Seehotel Appesbach

The Kozma's sturdy, yellow hotel with green shutters is a real oasis with a large garden, thick woods and the lake protecting it from the rather touristy resort of St. Wolfgang. Tennis, golf and sailing-school nearby. Above-average food.

■ 5360 St Wolfgang am Wolfgangsee **Tel** (06138) 2209 **Fax** (06138) 220914 **Meals** breakfast, lunch, dinner, snacks **Prices** rooms AS690-1400 with breakfast; meals from AS200 **Rooms** 28, all with bath or shower, central heating, phone **Credit cards** AE, DC, MC, V **Closed** hotel Nov to April; 5 apartments always open **Languages** English

Niederösterreich

Hotels in Lower Austria

Of the nine Federal States, Lower Austria is easily the biggest, even engulfing the newest, separate state of Vienna, its former capital. St Pölten is taking on the role of the administrative headquarters.

The River Danube splits the state in two, flowing from west to east. On the north bank is the Wachau, famous for the high quality of its wines, grown on steep hillsides between Melk and Krems.

A crescent of countryside to the west of Vienna itself is the famous *Wienerwald*, Vienna Woods, romanticized in waltz tunes and novels and still the area for the Viennese to enjoy a happy day out with a meal. Some might head for Gruberau and the Ulm family's modern restaurant with rooms, the Schusternazl (Tel (02238) 8226, fax 8451, 31 rooms).

For a more lavish meal, where reservations are essential, the Roten Wolf at Langenlebarn is rated among Austria's finest restaurants (Tel (02272) 2567, 17 rooms) and makes a pleasant overnight stay despite being near the railway station which, incidentally, runs to Vienna.

Another Vienna Woods favourite is the Jagdhof (Tel (02236) 52225, fax 5222540, 34 rooms) which has yet another fine and romantic restaurant, a mere 17 km from the Austrian capital. Food is also the attraction at Haus Bartberg in Pressbaum (Tel (02233) 27000, fax 27007, 13 rooms) where Ingrid Prechtl's cooking demands respect.

The Bocek-Faltus family runs the Marchfelderhof (Tel (02247) 2243, fax 223613, 15 rooms), yet another restaurant-with-rooms, this time in Deutsch Wagram, 19 km from Vienna.

Further away from the city is Eggenburg, medieval, pretty and popular with museum buffs who like prehistory or vintage motorcycles. The Stadthotel Eggenburg (Tel (02984) 3531, fax 3531101, 16 rooms) has a solid reputation for its cooking, with monthly gourmet food and wine evenings.

Across the Danube from Melk is the appropriately-named Melkerblick Hotel (Tel (02752) 7406, 30 rooms) in Emmersdorf, complete with ruined castle, while up in the quiet countryside near Bratislava, on the Czech border, is the Zur Goldenen Krone in Hainburg an der Donau (Tel (02165) 2105, 21 rooms).

For further details about the area, contact:
Niederösterreich-information,
Heidenschuss 2,
A-1010 Vienna.
Tel: (01) 5333114.
Fax: (01) 5350319.

This page acts as an introduction to the features and hotels of Lower Austria and gives brief recommendations of good hotels that for one reason or another have not made a full entry. The long entries for this state – covering the hotels we are most enthusiastic about – start on the next page. But do not neglect the shorter entries starting on page 119: these are all hotels that we would happily stay at.

Niederösterreich

Town hotel, Dürnstein

Gartenhotel Pfeffel

'Nice, jolly owner; nice, jolly place' ends our inspector's report on this inn, where oleanders, geraniums and a walnut tree add colour to the entrance. Situated just outside Dürnstein on the riverside road, our reporter warns would-be guests to take care since it is easy to miss the abrupt turning to the hotel under a railway arch. Although the building is modern, the general look is pleasantly old-fashioned. Where so many hotel dining-rooms in Austria are panelled in wood, this one has mirrors, making the small room look larger and providing a multi-reflection of the chandelier. The breakfast room is contemporary, with tiled floors, rush-seated chairs, and an open fireplace.

Views change with every flight of steps: the sitting area and terrace look out on the hills; some of the bedrooms face the Danube. All are spacious, with lace mats on the dark wood furniture. Like other hoteliers in this region, the Pfeffels have their own wine production, 'von den steilen Bergterassen des Schreiberberges' ('from the steep hanging terraces of the Schreiberberg' above them) and special dishes range from fish and lamb to nettle-cream soup.

Nearby Dürnstein; Danube; Wachau.

3601 Dürnstein
Tel (02711) 206
Fax (02711) 22888
Location along riverside from Dürnstein, abrupt turn under railway arch; ample car parking
Meals breakfast, lunch, dinner
Prices rooms AS560-1360 with breakfast; DB&B from AS700, reductions for children; meals from AS140
Rooms 33 double, 5 single; all have bath or shower, central heating, phone, TV, minibar, hairdrier
Facilities 2 dining-rooms, 3 sitting-rooms, bar, TV room, table-tennis room; terrace, sauna, small outdoor pool
Credit Cards DC, MC, V
Children welcome
Disabled not suitable
Pets accepted
Closed Nov to March
Languages English, French
Proprietors Pfeffel family

Niederösterreich

Gasthof Sänger Blondel

Everyone knows the legend of the minstrel, Blondel, who discovered the whereabouts of the imprisoned King Richard I of England by singing the monarch's favourite song beneath the castle battlements. Did it really happen? Who cares? The old walled town of Dürnstein and its ruined castle are still worth a visit, particularly when you stay in this yellow-painted villa.

The Schendls take great care over their food, not only following regional recipes, but using plenty of organic produce. Our inspector happily devoured home-made bread and apricot jam, plum dumplings and praline chocolates. The wine list, with its detailed descriptions, makes interesting reading and even better drinking. The family have been in Dürnstein for 300 years and have been inn-keepers since 1900. In this much-visited town it would be all too easy to rest on their laurels; fortunately they do not. Colours throughout tone with the caramel-coloured oak panelling, and the terrace garden is full of flowers. Looming above is the heavily-decorated blue tower of the *Stiftskirche*. Once a week there is an evening of zither music and there are bicycles for guests to use.

Nearby Dürnstein; Danube River; Wachau.

3601 Dürnstein
Tel (02711) 253
Fax (02711) 2537
Location in Dürnstein, not overlooking river; car parking outside, 4 garage spaces
Meals breakfast, lunch, dinner, snacks
Prices rooms AS630-1050 with breakfast; reductions for children; meals from AS200
Rooms 15 double, 1 single; all have bath or shower, central heating, phone, hairdrier

Facilities 3 dining-rooms, TV room; terrace
Credit Cards not accepted
Children accepted
Disabled not suitable
Pets accepted
Closed mid-Nov to end Feb
Languages English, French
Proprietors Schendl family

Niederösterreich

Converted granary, Geras

Alter Schüttkasten Geras

This former granary proves the theory that you can make an interesting hotel out of almost anything. Situated on the outskirts of the rather ordinary village of Geras, the massive structure dates from the 17thC when it was built to store grain for the nearby monastery, which still owns the property.

Walls are over one metre thick, roofs are steep, windows are small and the only decoration on the outside is a baroque stone Madonna. Luckily, the conversion to restaurant and hotel was sensitive; any temptation to over-furnish the rooms with plush curtains and fancy ornaments was resisted. The style remains simple, the atmosphere tranquil.

Hic habitat fortuna ('Here happiness reigns') reads the inscription in the lobby, where stark, white walls contrast with terracotta floor tiles. Bedrooms, with rush-seated chairs, crisp linens and a cross on the wall have 'a pleasingly puritanical look' according to our inspector. He also liked the vaulted cellars, which once held the monks' wine, but now have dining-tables and chairs. Menus offer game and fish from the monastery's estates. Book into summer painting courses through the hotel.

Nearby woods, hiking, painting holidays.

2093 Geras, Vorstadt 11
Tel (02912) 332
Fax (02912) 33233
Location on edge of town; ample car parking
Meals breakfast, lunch, dinner, snacks
Prices rooms AS520-800 with breakfast; DB&B from AS620; reduction for children; meals from AS95
Rooms 21 double, 5 single; all have bath or shower, central heating, phone, TV, minibar

Facilities 2 dining-rooms, bar, TV room; terrace
Credit Cards DC
Children welcome
Disabled reasonable access; lift/elevator
Pets accepted
Closed never
Languages English
Proprietor Monastery

Niederösterreich

Castle inn, Haitzendorf

Schlosstaverne Grafenegg

What happens when an Austrian meets a Belgian in Brazil? In the case of Wilhelm and Christiane Hüttl, they marry, move to Lower Austria and, ambitiously, open a small hotel. That was in 1991. The impressive 19thC Gothic-style Grafenegg Castle belongs to Duke Metternich-Sandor, so the Hüttls have leased the castle inn, which has a flair and elegance reminiscent of a French chateau. The castle itself is well known for its classical music concerts, which take place in the enormous indoor riding-school and feature soloists like Alfred Brendel, who played in 1992. Seminars and banquets are also popular.

Despite the grandeur of the complex, the Hüttls have created an aura of intimacy, with half a dozen rooms and personal service. Candle-lit dining in the aptly-named Green Salon is already gaining a following. Bedrooms have pretty floral wallpaper in Laura Ashley style, corridors are lined with 19thC etchings by Caspar David Friedrich.

Our inspector admits that this hotel is "a little out-of-the-way", even though it is only 12 km from Krems, but praises the Hüttls for their enthusiasm.

Nearby Krems; Danube River; Wachau; vineyards.

3485 Haitzendorf, Grafenegg 12
Tel (02735) 2616
Fax (02735) 758420
Location in countryside, near village of Haitzendorf; ample car parking
Meals breakfast, lunch, dinner, snacks
Prices AS500-730 with breakfast, reduction for children; meals from AS250
Rooms 7 double; all have bath or shower, central heating, phone, radio; TV on request; minibar in corridor
Facilities 3 dining-rooms, bar; terrace
Credit Cards not accepted
Children accepted
Disabled not suitable
Pets accepted
Closed mid-Dec to Feb
Languages English, French, Dutch, Portuguese
Managers Hüttl family

Niederösterreich

Village inn, Hinterbrühl

Die Höldrichsmühle

This is where Schubert was supposedly inspired to write one of his most famous songs, *Der Lindenbaum*. The ancient lime, or linden, tree was later destroyed by lightning but Schubert's portrait still graces the doorway. He was not the only artist to enjoy hospitality here; Beethoven stayed, as did painter Georg Waldmüller and playwright Ferdinand Raimund. The history of the building is even older than its 200 years as an inn; farmers came to this mill to grind grain as far back as 1210.

Nowadays, this is an attractive and well-run village inn. In fine weather, meals are served in the garden, shaded by chestnut trees. Otherwise there is a formal dining-room upstairs and intimate little *Stüberln* downstairs. Only 17 km from Vienna, it is popular both at weekends and for weekday business lunches. Bedrooms, however, are rather small for the price, and struck us as impersonal. The road in front is a main one, so ask for a room at the back to be sure of a quiet night. Those who have been riding through the Wienerwald presumably sleep well; the stables and riding school are right on the premises. As for pets, the two resident cocker spaniels only accept dogs smaller than themselves.

Nearby Heiligenkreuz; Vienna Woods; riding, tennis.

2371 Hinterbrühl, Gaadnerstr 34
Tel (02236) 262740
Fax (02236) 48729
Location in Vienna Woods village, 17 km from Vienna; ample car-parking
Meals breakfast, lunch, dinner, snacks
Prices rooms AS750-1250 with breakfast; DB&B from AS970; reduction for children; meals from AS200
Rooms 19 double; all have bath or shower, central heating, phone, TV, minibar, hairdrier
Facilities 5 dining-rooms; terrace
Credit Cards AE, DC, MC, V
Children welcome
Disabled reasonable access, ground floor bedrooms
Pets accepted if not too big
Closed 2 weeks in Feb
Languages English, French, Italian, Hungarian
Proprietors Moser family

Niederösterreich

Country restaurant with rooms, Klein Wien

Landgasthof Schickh

A 'restaurant and hotel next to the railway station' did not sound like a promising candidate, so we were surprised by the headline on our inspector's report: 'Triple A rating'. His comments were littered with exclamation marks – for the food, the surroundings and the professional yet friendly host. The building is low, painted yellow and right next to the single-track Krems-St. Pölten line, 'mercifully silent at night and with very little traffic during the day' although there is the occasional blast from a locomotive. Railway buffs insist on having bedrooms overlooking the line. Everyone, however, likes to have a drink in the 80-year old railway carriage in the garden, furnished to resemble a Viennese café.

All three dining-rooms are attractive, although different in size and decoration. Regulars, including the Viennese acting fraternity, book tables in the one which suits their mood. They also sit out in the large garden, shaded by horse chestnut trees. This is where the house specialties, lobster and crayfish, are kept alive in tanks. Other dishes getting rave reviews include: trout *en gelée*, duck breast with cheese and garlic noodles, and apricot dumplings, 'the best in Austria.'

Nearby Stift Göttweig monastery.

3511 Klein Wien, Furth-Göttweig
Tel (02736) 218
Fax (02736) 2187
Location beneath hill-top monastery of Göttweig; ample car parking
Meals breakfast, lunch, dinner, snacks
Prices rooms AS500-800 with breakfast; DB&B from AS750; reduction for children; meals from AS250
Rooms 9 double, 2 single, 1 apartment; all have bath and shower, central heating, phone, TV, radio
Facilities 4 dining-rooms, bar; railway-carriage diner
Credit Cards not accepted
Children welcome
Disabled not suitable
Pets accepted
Closed never; restaurant only, Wed, Thurs
Languages English, French
Proprietor Ferdinand Schickh

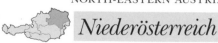

Niederösterreich

Restaurant with rooms, Krems/Donau

Am Förthof

'Superb wine list' and 'fabulous desserts' were our inspector's comments on Helga Figl's well-known restaurant. The wide range of wines by the glass and the knowledgeable wine-waiter make this an oenophile's delight. The chefs, too, clearly know their business, although hearty appetites might find the portions a little scant.

Unfortunately, the same high ratings could not be given for the decoration of the public rooms. Frau Figl, who also runs a coffee and wine business in Dürnstein, took over her parents' business in 1991 and is slowly updating this 200-year old former hunting lodge. Already the bedrooms have been refurbished successfully, in white with pastel blue, pink, green or yellow. The new suites are stylish also, with Biedermeier furniture. We hope that the improvements will extend soon to the rest of the hotel. Frau Figl encourages local artists by displaying their work and there is even a huge painting on an easel near reception. You may, or may not, like what is on show when you visit. Week-long programmes are offered, with lectures and tours on themes of churches, castles, museums, and wine.

Nearby Krems and Stein old towns; wine museum; Dürnstein.

3504 Krems, Donaulände 8
Tel (02732) 83345
Fax (02732) 8334540
Location on road looking south over Danube; car-parking outside
Meals breakfast, lunch, dinner, snacks
Prices AS650-1050 with breakfast; DB&B from AS950; reduction for children; meals from AS300
Rooms 20 double, 2 suites; all have bath or shower, central heating, phone, TV, radio
Facilities 2 dining-rooms, TV room; terrace, small outdoor swimming-pool
Credit Cards DC, MC, V
Children accepted
Disabled not suitable
Pets accepted
Closed never
Languages English, French, Italian
Proprietor Helga Figl

Niederösterreich

❃ **Health farm, Lackenhof** ❃

Biohotel Jagdhof

You do not have to take the cure to feel healthy here; just gazing on meadows, hills and woods is therapeutic for city folk. The 20-year old building was remodelled in 1990 and is now a *Biohotel*. This means that natural fibres and materials are used in furnishings and a masterswitch in bedrooms can cut off all electrical current while guests sleep.

Frau Borbath is in charge of the kitchen; her motto is 'natural and light', with an emphasis on whole-food menus incorporating plenty of organic fruit and vegetables. Although she is an enthusiast for the healthy way of eating, she is no dietary despot; regional specialities are also offered, plus home-made breads and herb *Schnaps*. The *Biostub'n* is a no-smoking zone, as are the Tower Suites and one entire floor of bedrooms. Fitness fans swim in the heated outdoor swimming-pool, play tennis on the clay court, practice golf shots on the driving range and hike the 150 km of marked trails. Fly-fishing, para-gliding and river-rafting can be arranged. In winter, the ski-lift on Ötscher mountain is just 150 m away. We would be happy to stay put and have massages, cosmetic treatments and spa baths.

Nearby hiking, tennis, golf; winter sports.

3295 Lackenhof am Ötscher, Weitental 95
Tel (07480) 3000
Fax (07480) 3008
Location in meadows at foot of Ötscher mountain; ample car parking
Meals breakfast, lunch, dinner, snacks
Prices AS620-1600 with breakfast; reductions for children; meals from AS200
Rooms 16 double, 3 single, 4 suites for 4-6 people; all have bath or shower, central heating, phone, TV, radio
Facilities 3 dining-rooms, sitting-room, bar; terrace, gymnasium, health spa, heated outdoor swimming-pool, garden
Credit Cards AE, DC, MC, V
Children welcome
Disabled not suitable
Pets accepted **Closed** 2 weeks Nov; 2 weeks after Easter
Languages English, French
Proprietors Borbath family

Niederösterreich

Restaurant with rooms, Mayerling

Hotel Marienhof

The Kronprinz is one of Austria's top 50 restaurants. Its name reflects the continuing fascination for the mysterious and tragic suicide pact between Crown Prince Rudolf and the beautiful Baroness Marie Vetsera. It all happened 100 years ago at the royal hunting-lodge in nearby Mayerling. Nowadays, the Marienhof's high prices may promote suicidal tendences among ordinary folk but they do not seem to deter business clients from driving the 30 km out of Vienna for small seminars and fine food in stylish surroundings.

Chestnut and lime (or linden) trees surround the hotel, which was once an inn for the famous monastery in Heiligenkreuz, not far away. Travellers of old would be astounded by the spacious bedrooms, each with a whirlpool bath, let alone the creations of chef Heinz-Viktor Hanner. He acknowledges the influence of France while using the finest ingredients such as salmon, venison and crayfish. No detail is overlooked: herbs are grown in his own garden, the wine list runs to 200 vintages from France, Spain, Italy and Austria, and there is even a *Käse-Somelier* who selects cheeses for ripening in a special cellar.

Nearby tennis; riding; Heiligenkreuz.

2534 Mayerling 1
Tel (02258) 23784
Fax (02258) 237941
Location in country between Mayerling and Heiligenkreuz; ample car parking
Meals breakfast, lunch, dinner, snacks
Prices AS750-1880 with breakfast; DB&B from AS970; reduction for children; meals from AS150
Rooms 23 double, 5 single, 4 suites; all have bath or shower, central heating, phone, TV, minibar, radio
Facilities 3 dining-rooms, bar; terrace; gymnasium, health spa
Credit Cards AE
Children welcome
Disabled not suitable
Pets accepted
Closed never
Languages English, French, Italian
Proprietors Hanner family

Niederösterreich

Castle hotel, Mühldorf

Burg Oberrana

Special experiences rarely come cheaply, but this one is worth every penny. The Nemetz family rescued this romantic, Renaissance castle from dilapidation a decade ago. Standing on a hill above the Danube valley, a castellated wall protects the 900-year old building with its steep grey roofs, sheer white walls and windows high above ground level. The crypt beneath the handsome, Romanesque chapel is 200 years older; the oldest, in fact, in Austria. Oberrana is secluded, with views to every point of the compass over wooded hills, valleys and pasture. The interior has been sympathetically restored, the beamed ceilings and white arches balanced by thick Persian carpets and clusters of pictures, a traditional *Kachelofen* and a grandfather clock.

Bedrooms and suites have well-chosen antique furniture; one of the best is the single with a four-poster baroque bed, curtained in green. Bathrooms are rather small, perhaps because of the difficulty in building them into such a massive structure. We would happily while away the time watching deer grazing in the inner moat while sipping one of the manager's home made apple or apricot brandies.

Nearby Wachauer Tal, Krems.

3622 Mühldorf bei Spitz/
Donau
Tel (02713) 8221
Fax (02713) 8366
Location on crest of hill above
village; ample car parking
Meals breakfast, snacks
Prices rooms AS530-1200
with breakfast; reductions for
children
Rooms 7 suites, 4 double, 1
single; all have bath or shower,
central heating, phone, TV,
radio

Facilities breakfast room,
sitting-room, bar, TV room;
terrace, garden
Credit Cards AE, V
Children very welcome
Disabled not suitable
Pets accepted
Closed 1 Nov to 1 May
Languages English
Managers Stierschneider
family
Proprietors Nemetz family

Niederösterreich

Riverside inn, Raabs an der Thaya

Hotel Thaya

Any hotel on the banks of a river, overlooking an 11thC castle, has to have a head start over its rivals. Raabs itself is a sleepy little village in what many Austrians consider to be a backwater, bordering Czechoslovakia. The squat yellow inn dates from 1890. From the main street, guests step straight into the bustling *Stüberl*, which our inspector thinks has 'a slightly French brasserie air about it,' perhaps because of the old lithographs in art nouveau frames. The smaller dining room has pine-framed booths with green velvet cushions. In the larger restaurant, a mural depicts costumed villagers from 1300 to 1900.

The bedrooms are in the new addition, built in 1988. Picture windows look over the garden, or even better, lead on to balconies overhanging the river itself. Decoration is simple in cool greys and whites; bathrooms are compact but practical.

This is a sports-oriented hotel, with canoeing on the still, green Thaya River. Franz Strohmer leads trips himself and also takes guests on excursions into Czechoslovakia. Cooking is above average, with hearty local dishes plus international favourites.

Nearby Raabs Castle, Rosenburg falconry; water-sports, tennis, riding, squash.

3820 Raabs an der Thaya
Tel (02846) 202
Fax (02846) 33225
Location on main street of village, overlooking river; own car parking
Meals breakfast, lunch, dinner, snacks
Prices AS350-660 with breakfast; DB&B from AS450; reductions for children
Rooms 27 double, 3 apartments; all have shower, central heating

Facilities 3 dining-rooms, sitting-room, bar, TV room; terrace; gymnasium, sauna
Credit Cards not accepted
Children very welcome
Disabled not suitable
Pets accepted with advance notice
Closed March
Languages English
Proprietors Strohmer family

Niederösterreich

Knappenhof

Our inspector thoroughly enjoyed the drive from Reichenau, up a narrow road through pastures and orchards, to this hotel. Built in 1907, it stands on the southern slopes of the Rax. Fresh flowers and a large wrought-iron chandelier dominate the entrance-hall and big wooden peasant chests stand in corridors. Bedrooms are in relaxing shades of pale blue or pink, with white walls covered in pictures of mountains. Two rooms at the back are rather gloomy; the rest have splendid views.

Kurhotels sometimes have a rather austere atmosphere, as if healthy regimes preclude enjoyment, particularly where food is concerned. Angela Puskas has other ideas and her award-winning food wins converts because it is imaginative and full of both flavour and variety. Butter, oil and cream are avoided. Instead, herbs and other natural flavourings are used to enhance fish, meat and organic vegetables. Even wild rice is prepared like an Italian risotto. The hotel also boasts a non-smoking dining-room. This is where Angela keeps her family of teddy bears, a collection that has grown since childhood. She also owns the popular 'Push In' wine-bar in Vienna.

Nearby tennis, riding, hunting; cable-car to Rax Alps.

2651 Reichenau, Kleinau 34
Tel (02666) 3633
Fax (02666) 363310
Location on southern slopes of Rax; ample car parking
Meals breakfast, lunch, dinner, snacks
Prices AS420-1100 with breakfast; DB&B from AS520; reduction for children; meals from AS150
Rooms 14 double, 4 single, 1 suite; all have bath or shower, central heating, phone, TV, radio
Facilities 3 dining-rooms, 2 sitting-rooms, TV room; terrace; gymnasium, health spa
Credit Cards DC, V
Children welcome
Disabled limited facilities
Pets accepted
Closed never
Languages English, French, Italian
Proprietors Drs. Braun, Angela Puskas

Niederösterreich

Castle hotel, near Zwettl

Schloss Rosenau

This small, baroque mansion, complete with clock tower, nestles in a small wooded valley near the Czech border. It is only 10 km from Zwettl but our inspector needed a good map to find it. Rose bushes and statuary line the approach, while inside every inch of wall space is decorated, every alcove bears a fresco. In contrast, bedrooms are nearly unadorned; some have heavy, dark furniture, others have honey-coloured pine beds, but all have plain white walls. Chef Anton Barth is building quite a reputation for his Waldviertel specialities such as local lamb and game, often combined with berries and mushrooms in the autumn. Earlier in the season, our inspector enjoyed fresh asparagus and shrimp soup and deep-fried elderflowers but was disappointed by the more basic dumplings.

He was completely taken aback, however, by the museum of freemasonry, the only one in Europe. It is an authentic 18thC lodge, complete with symbols and regalia. All quite a contrast to the indoor swimming-pool, mini-golf and tennis-courts. 'A classy establishment but not as expensive as one might expect,' he writes, impressed that five bedrooms can take wheelchairs.
Nearby tennis, fishing, riding.

3924 Schloss Rosenau, bei Zwettl
Tel (02822) 58221
Fax (02822) 582218
Location deep in country, near Zwettl; ample car parking
Meals breakfast, lunch, dinner, snacks
Prices rooms AS640-1300 with breakfast; meals from AS130
Rooms 13 double, 4 single; all have bath or shower, central heating, phone, TV, radio

Facilities 3 dining-rooms, TV room, sauna, indoor swimming-pool
Credit Cards not accepted
Children very welcome
Disabled recommended; 5 bedrooms accessible
Pets accepted
Closed mid-Jan to mid-March
Languages English, French
Manager Gerhard Hahn

Niederösterreich

Village inn, Weissenkirchen

Raffelsbergerhof

A gem, pure and simple. Who would not want to stay in this late-Renaissance house on the edge of the village? Turn off the main street down a little lane towards the Danube and suddenly you are in a flower-filled square. Wistaria and vines climb over this former ship-master's house, where the stables once housed the horses that pulled the Danube barges upstream.

Outside, a statue of St. John of Nepomuk stands in a small niche; inside, a stern stone face spouts water into a tiny pool and ancient steps lead up to reception. Claudia Anton is the second generation of her family to run this pension. Her antique-dealer father restored the 16thC building, then filled it with eye-catching objects. In the breakfast room, a Biedermeier cabinet displays gold-embroidered *Wachauer Hauben,* the traditional bonnets of the region. Even the locks, handles, hinges and light fittings are finely-crafted and worthy of notice. Views from the vaulted rooms and arcades are either into the garden with its walnut and cherry trees or out towards the late-Gothic church and hills. Bedrooms are attractively-furnished with modern bathrooms; two have views of the Danube.

Nearby church; Wachau Museum.

3610 Weissenkirchen
Tel (02715) 2201
Fax (02715) 220127
Location on edge of village, overlooking square; own car parking
Meals breakfast
Prices AS500-1300 with breakfast; reductions for children
Rooms 12 double, 1 single; all have bath or shower, central heating, phone, TV, minibar, radio; some have hairdrier

Facilities breakfast room
Credit Cards MC
Children accepted
Disabled not suitable
Pets not accepted
Closed Nov to end April
Languages English, Italian
Proprietor Claudia Anton

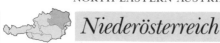

Niederösterreich

Village inn, Ysper

Zum Grünen Baum

Many hotels boast of having a 'long tradition of hospitality'; this one offers public proof. A scrolled plaque on the wall bears the date of foundation: 1648. Even without that, the ancient beams, low ceilings, and walls one metre thick bear witness to its age. Not only has this been a coaching inn for all those years, the ownership has passed down through generations of the same family. 'Almost an agricultural museum' wrote our inspector, as he noted the carriage shafts and yokes, rakes and wheels hung on the white-washed walls. The atmosphere, however, is not staid; children are very welcome because 'after all, we're a family ourselves'.

In the *Stüberl,* walls are decorated with embroidered peasant sayings and a target used by hunters for shooting practice. Traditional recipes feature on the large menu, with herbs and vegetables direct from their own garden.

The Rotters have kept up with the times, however, adding a new wing in 1978. Bedrooms here are decorated in light blue, green or grey, with pale pine furniture, compared to the darker look of the older bedrooms. The village, too, is delightfully unspoiled; it even has its own pillory.

Nearby hiking, riding, fishing, tennis.

3683 Ysper
Tel (07415) 218
Fax (07415) 21849
Location in middle of charming village; car parking on village square
Meals breakfast, lunch, dinner
Prices rooms AS440-700 with breakfast, DB&B from AS540, reductions for children, meals from AS100
Rooms 29 double, 5 single; all have bath or shower, central heating, phone, TV

Facilities 3 dining-rooms, sitting-room, bar; 2 terraces, garden; sauna
Credit Cards not accepted
Children very welcome
Disabled not suitable
Pets accepted
Closed 2 weeks Feb; 1 week Nov
Languages English
Proprietors Rotter family

Niederösterreich

Village guest-house, Artstetten

Gasthof Landstetter

This cheerful, 100-year old hotel is on a rise above a village famous for its castle. Huge chestnut trees guard the door; bedrooms are large, with majestic views over the countryside. The Landstetters enjoy playing folk-music for their guests.

■ 3661 Artstetten **Tel** (07413) 8303 **Meals** breakfast, lunch, dinner, snacks **Prices** rooms AS270-620 with breakfast; meals from AS110 **Rooms** 28, all with bath or shower, central heating, radio; TV on request **Credit cards** not accepted **Closed** Jan to Easter **Languages** English

---

Converted villa, Baden

Pension Almschlössl

Only a 10-minute walk from the middle of the old-fashioned spa of Baden, this Mediterranean-style villa has a large garden with panoramic views of the town. Bedrooms are pretty in pastel blues, with green shutters. Covered garage space.

■ 2500 Baden, Alm 1 **Tel** (02252) 48240 **Meals** breakfast, snacks **Prices** rooms AS400-1100 with breakfast **Rooms** 7, all with bath or shower, central heating, TV **Credit cards** not accepted **Closed** Nov to Easter **Languages** English

---

Country mansion, Dörfl

Pedro's Landhaus

Palatial, plush and pricey, this joint-venture by Pedro Massana and fellow-Spaniard and opera star José Carreras is set in a huge park. More like a country club in the Vienna Woods, with no expense spared on carpets, curtains, furniture.

■ 3072 Dörfl, Kasten **Tel** (02744) 7387 **Fax** (02744) 7389 **Meals** breakfast, lunch, dinner, snacks **Prices** rooms AS950-1400 with breakfast; meals from AS400 **Rooms** 11, all with bath or shower, central heating, phone, TV **Credit cards** MC **Closed** never **Languages** English, French, Italian, Spanish

---

Castle hotel, Drosendorf

Schloss Drosendorf

A romantic, Renaissance castle where nobility once stayed, this is now in real need of restoration. In a backwater, near the Czech border. Experience rambling rooms, antique and modern furniture, but don't expect to be pampered.

■ 2095 Drosendorf, Schlossplatz 1 **Tel** (029152) 3210 **Fax** (029152) 32140 **Meals** breakfast; small tavern next door **Prices** rooms AS330-600 with breakfast **Rooms** 21, all with bath or shower, central heating, TV **Credit cards** not accepted **Closed** last week Dec **Languages** English, French, Italian

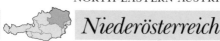

Niederösterreich

Village inn, Göstling an der Ybbs

Zum Goldenen Hirschen

Next to the Gothic/baroque church, this 550-year old, vine-covered inn is ideal for an overnight stop in this delightful village with its Renaissance houses. The old *Stube* has chandeliers made of antlers; practical, modern bedrooms.

■ 3345 Göstling an der Ybbs 16 **Tel** (07484) 2225 **Fax** (07484) 222528 **Meals** breakfast, lunch, dinner, snacks **Prices** rooms AS380-840 with breakfast; meals from AS100 **Rooms** 18, all with shower, central heating, phone, TV, radio **Credit cards** V **Closed** Nov **Languages** English, French

---

Former medieval house, Klosterneuburg

Appartement-hotel Schrannenhof

In the heart of town, the Veit family owns a restaurant, bed-and-breakfast and this small hotel. Carefully converted in 1990, it retains the old arched ceilings and stone floors and has apartments with large bedrooms and small kitchens.

■ 3400 Klosterneuburg, Niedermarkt 17-19 **Tel** (02243) 2072 **Fax** (02243) 207213 **Meals** breakfast **Prices** rooms AS700-1100 with breakfast; meals from AS150 **Rooms** 13, all with bath or shower, central heating, phone, TV, kitchenette **Credit cards** not accepted **Closed** never **Languages** English, French, Italian

---

Old farmhouse, Kronberg am Russbach

Landhaus Kronberghof

The Grossauer family keeps both horse riders and diners happy. With 70 horses and an indoor school, there is an authentic rustic atmosphere, deep in the country. Brigitte Grossauer's cooking concentrates on local Waldviertel dishes.

■ 2123 Kronberg am Russbach 3 **Tel** (02245) 4304 **Fax** (02245) 5497 **Meals** breakfast, lunch, dinner, snacks **Prices** rooms AS380-760 with breakfast; meals from AS85 **Rooms** 5, all with bath or shower, central heating, phone, TV **Credit cards** not accepted **Closed** restaurant only, Mon, Tues **Languages** English, French, Italian

---

Restaurant with rooms, Laaben

Landgasthof Zur Linde

In a charming village in the Vienna Woods, the Stohrs' restaurant is a regular draw for the Viennese who sit in the garden or old *Stube*. Less well-known are the practical bedrooms in the new block next door. Special weekend packages.

■ 3053 Laaben 28, im Wienerwald **Tel** (02774) 8378 **Fax** (02774) 837820 **Meals** breakfast, lunch, dinner, snacks **Prices** rooms AS350-640 with breakfast; meals from AS100 **Rooms** 14, all with bath or shower, central heating, phone, TV **Credit cards** not accepted **Closed** mid-Nov to mid-Dec; 2 weeks in March; restaurant only, Wed **Languages** German only

Niederösterreich

Restaurant with rooms, Mautern

Landhaus Bacher

Lisl Wagner-Bacher is among Austria's top dozen chefs, so her restaurant, in the middle of a pretty village, is a high temple of cuisine. Rooms in the hotel are very feminine in soft creams and greys. Service may be somewhat haughty.

■ 3512 Mautern, Südtirolerplatz **Tel** (02732) 82937 **Fax** (02732) 74337 **Meals** breakfast, lunch, dinner, snacks **Prices** rooms AS700-1750 with breakfast; meals from AS300 **Rooms** 11, all with bath or shower, central heating, phone, TV, minibar, hairdrier **Credit cards** not accepted **Closed** end Jan to end Feb **Languages** English, French

---

Converted villa, Payerbach

Alpenhof

Architecture fans will appreciate this villa, designed by Adolf Loos 60 years ago. This early example of modern functionalism, with dark-stained wooden furniture, has been altered little. A hideaway for Viennese. Steep approach; dramatic views.

■ 2650 Payerbach **Tel** (02666) 2911 **Meals** breakfast, lunch, dinner, snacks **Prices** rooms AS240-300 with breakfast; meals from AS150 **Rooms** 14, all with bath or shower, central heating; TV on request **Credit cards** not accepted **Closed** never **Languages** English

---

❋   Town inn, Puchberg am Schneeberg   ❋

Puchbergerhof

Five minutes' walk from the old steam cog railway that goes up the Schneeberg, this 17thC inn is right in town, yet quiet. Ask for a room with a balcony overlooking the garden. Food is filling rather than exciting; vegetarian dishes offered.

■ 2734 Puchberg am Schneeberg, Wiener-Neustädterstr 29 **Tel** (02636) 2278 **Meals** breakfast, lunch, dinner **Prices** rooms AS240-580 with breakfast; meals from AS120 **Rooms** 23, all with bath or shower, phone **Credit Cards** not accepted **Closed** Nov to mid-Dec **Languages** English, some French

---

❋   Restaurant with rooms, Semmering   ❋

Hotel Belvedere

The main draw is not the decoration, but rather the excellent cuisine and welcome from Magda and Karl Engelschall. Desserts in the sunny restaurant are wonderful as the family trained with Demel in Vienna. Large swimming-pool. Ski-lifts 5 minutes.

■ 2680 Semmering, Hochstr 60 **Tel** (02664) 270267 **Fax** (02664) 26742 **Meals** breakfast, lunch, dinner, snacks **Prices** rooms AS300-1100 with breakfast; meals from AS180 **Rooms** 19, all with bath or shower, central heating, phone, TV, radio **Credit cards** AE, DC, MC, V **Closed** Nov **Languages** English, some French, Italian

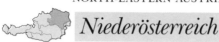

Niederösterreich

❊   Forest hotel, Semmering   ❊

Pension Daheim

This brown, wooden inn with green shutters dates from 1913. Built on a hillside among pine-trees, its large terrace has sweeping views of the Rax Alps. Cosy inside, with striking curved bannisters, pleasant bedrooms. Viennese-style cooking.

■ 2680 Semmering **Tel** (02664) 382 **Fax** (02664) 38177 **Meals** breakfast, lunch, dinner, snacks **Prices** rooms AS260-660 with breakfast **Rooms** 12, all with bath or shower, central heating, phone; TV on request **Credit cards** not accepted **Closed** end Oct to mid-Dec; 10 days after Easter **Languages** English, French

---

Modern country hotel, Tullnerbach

Pension Wittman-Wienerwaldblick

An unpretentious, homely retreat in the Vienna Woods, overlooking orchards and valley. The Wittmans are especially hospitable. Decor is rather 1970s, plain and dark. Own lamb, local cheeses on menu. Big terrace. Only 20 km west of Vienna.

■ 3011 Untertullnerbach, Irenental, Brettwieserstr 33 **Tel** (02233) 2147 **Fax** (02233) 21476 **Meals** breakfast, lunch, dinner, snacks **Prices** rooms AS300-600 with breakfast; meals from AS120 **Rooms** 7, all with bath or shower, central heating, phone; TV in 2 rooms **Credit cards** not accepted **Closed** last 2 weeks Nov **Languages** English

---

Country inn, Weistrach

Landgasthof Kirchmayr

Weistrach is a delightful village and the Kirchmayr's solid, mustard-coloured country inn is a focal point. As the family's wine business is just across the street, one hundred wines are on offer in the gourmet restaurant. Some simple rooms.

■ 3351 Weistrach, Haus 9 **Tel** (07477) 2380 **Meals** breakfast, lunch, dinner, snacks **Prices** rooms AS250-560 with breakfast; meals from AS200 **Rooms** 4, all with bath or shower, central heating, phone **Credit cards** not accepted **Closed** one week March; restaurant only Mon, Tues **Languages** English

---

Village inn, Ysper

Zur Blauen Traube

In one of Austria's prettiest villages, this typical, pink-painted, Waldviertel inn celebrated its 250th birthday in 1992. Guests dine out in a courtyard full of creepers and geraniums. They also relax in the garden and play skittles in the bar.

■ 3683 Ysper 31 **Tel** (07415) 265 **Meals** breakfast, lunch, dinner, snacks **Prices** rooms AS280-520 with breakfast; meals from AS100 **Rooms** 18, all with bath or shower, central heating, phone **Credit cards** not accepted **Closed** Nov to Easter **Languages** English

Vienna

Hotels in Vienna

As one of the world's most popular cities for tourists, Vienna is crammed with hotels ranging from 5-star magnificence to the simplest private rooms. All are used year-round, so staff and furnishings are tested to the limit.

Most famous is, arguably, the legendary Sacher. Large, lush and home to the rich and famous, the Sacher is opposite the Opera House. Even if you cannot afford to stay here, you can always visit the coffee house to order a slice of the chocolate cake that is synonymous with the hotel: Sachertorte. (Tel (0222) 514560, fax 51457810, 117 rooms).

A ten-minute walk from the middle of the city is another legend, the Palais Schwarzenberg (Tel (0222) 784515, fax 784714, 38 rooms), part of the 17thC palace. About a quarter of the rooms overlook the exquisite formal gardens; antiques and chandeliers abound for visitors looking for 'an experience'.

Another 5-star hotel with splendid views is the Clima Villenhotel, about 8 km from the middle of Vienna, set among the vineyards of Nussdorf. The cellar-bar is old and romantic. The hotel itself is modern, concrete, functional and, by Austria's charming standards, lacks character (Tel (0222) 371516, fax 371392, 30 rooms).

Back in the city, on a more modest note, are several small hotels and *Pensions* which appeal to the budget-conscious. In the south-east, overlooking the Ringstrasse, the Arenberg offers a warm welcome from staff who are commendably cheerful, considering the steady stream of tourists that cross their threshhold. (Tel (0222) 5125291, fax 5139356, 20 rooms).

The Familien-Hotel St James is very Austrian, with plenty of business regulars. Despite a good deal of charm, the hotel is 'decidedly spartan', according to our inspector (Tel (0222) 5872408, fax 5876609, 25 rooms).

A useful base in the Josefstadt, a fashionable old quarter known for its baroque houses and numerous restaurants, is the Hotel Concordia (Tel (0222) 401180, fax 4011871, 27 rooms).

In addition to the hotels reviewed in the next 10 pages, for the convenience of our readers, we have also compiled a list of the charming small hotels that are within 80 km/1 hour's drive of Vienna. See the bottom of page 132.

For further details about the city, contact:
Wiener Tourismusverband,
Obere Augartenstr 40,
A-1025 Wien.
Tel (01) 211140.
Fax (01) 2168492.

This page acts as an introduction to the features and hotels of Vienna and gives brief recommendations of good hotels that for one reason or another have not made a full entry. The long entries for this state – covering the hotels we are most enthusiastic about – start on the next page. But do not neglect the shorter entries starting on page 132: these are all hotels that we would happily stay at.

Vienna

Town hotel

Altstadt Vienna

Owner Otto Ernst Wiesenthal spent 20 years travelling the world, so he knows what he likes and dislikes about hotels. When he took over this one (formerly the Bellaria), he changed the name and upgraded the furnishings. Now antiques mix harmoniously with modern furnishings in rooms with high ceilings and parquet floors. There is a sense of space throughout, particularly in the seating area which is large enough for a dance routine by Wiesenthal's famous ancestor, Grete, the Isadora Duncan of turn-of-the-century Vienna.

You get the feeling that the Wiesenthal family, which includes a pretty niece, enjoy playing host. Nothing seems to be too much trouble, whether it is providing a typewriter, a limousine from the airport or concert tickets.

The hotel occupies the upper stories of a wealthy burgher's house in Josefstadt, a well-preserved baroque quarter of the city that is quiet and residential but only 10 minutes by bus from the Ringstrasse. Bedrooms are high enough for roof-top views across to the tower of the nearby St Ulrich's church or towards the western Wienerwald.

Nearby Ulrichsplatz.

1070 Wien, Kirchengasse 41
Tel (01) 52633990
Fax (01) 5234901
Location in attractive street off Burggasse
Meals breakfast
Prices rooms 850-1750 with breakfast; children up to 6 free in parents' room
Rooms 23 double, 13 with bath and shower, 10 with shower; 2 single with shower; all rooms have central heating, phone, TV, minibar, hairdrier, radio

Facilities sitting room, opera ticket reservations
Credit Cards AE, DC, MC, V
Children welcome
Disabled not suitable
Pets accepted
Closed never
Languages English, Italian
Proprietor Otto Ernst Wiesenthal

Vienna

City hotel

Altwienerhof

Don't be put off by the unfashionable location, south of the Westbahnhof in an unattractive part of town: the Altwienerhof is a gem. Its restaurant, rated one of the best, if not the best, in Vienna, attracts local gourmets as well as foreigners, especially the French. The ever-changing menu focuses on fish, but baby lamb and potato strudel are also specialties; the wine list, with French classics and Austrian vintages, also receives rave reviews.

Chef Rudolf Kellner met his wife in London, where he trained at the Savoy Hotel, and together they have created an atmosphere of intimacy and luxury, both in the alcoves of the restaurant and in the hotel itself. The best bedrooms echo the *belle époque*, with plush velvet and lace, though gilded taps in the en suite marble bathrooms may be too much for conservative tastes. Note that lower-priced rooms taken with half-pension are a bargain. Breakfast in the conservatory or during warm weather in the garden, sheltered by cascades of ivy.

A warning to those on slimming diets: the smell of delicious food permeates the premises and piques the appetite.
Nearby Haydn Museum.

1150 Wien, Herklotzgasse 6
Tel (01) 8926000
Fax (01) 8926008
Location near Westbahnhof; own garage
Meals breakfast, lunch, dinner, snacks
Prices rooms AS480-1600 with breakfast, DB&B (for one) from AS730; children under 6 free, AS200 extra bed; meals from AS250
Rooms 9 double, 1 with bath, 8 with shower; 9 single, 2 with shower and WC, 4 showers only; 5 suites with bath; all have central heating, phone, TV
Facilities dining room, breakfast room, conservatory, terrace
Credit Cards V
Children welcome
Disabled not suitable
Pets accepted **Closed** never; restaurant 1 Jan to 21 Jan
Languages English, French, Italian **Proprietors** Rudolf and Ursula Kellner

Vienna

Wine-village pension

Landhaus Fuhrgassl-Huber

Opened in 1991, this *pension* immediately made a name for itself among local connoisseurs of small hotels. Set in the long, rather straggly wine-village of Neustift am Walde, it backs on to a slope covered by orderly rows of vines. Here is your chance to drink wine straight from the vineyard of one of Vienna's most famous *Heurigen*, the Fuhrgassl-Huber which just happens to be owned by the same family and is just down the street.

In contrast to the historic *Heurigen*, this hotel is a refreshing combination of old and new. Outside, the cream and white façade is ablaze with azaleas in spring; inside, antique hand-painted peasant wardrobes from the Tyrol catch the eye.

Our inspector enthused about the light and airy atmosphere, created by large windows looking into the courtyard (where guests can breakfast in summer) or out on to the garden. Flowers are everywhere, brightening the natural wood and tiled floors. Bedrooms are generous and comfortable, mainly pristine white, with curtains in clear greens or pinks.

Although central Vienna is only half an hour by bus and tram, the bustle of city life seems further away.

Nearby vineyards, Heurigen villages, Vienna Woods.

1190 Wien, Neustift am Walde, Rathstr 24
Tel (0222) 443033
Fax (0222) 442714
Location on main street of picturesque wine village, outskirts of Vienna; own garage
Meals breakfast, snacks
Prices rooms AS960-1470 with breakfast; children under 6 free; extra bed in room AS360
Rooms 22 double; all have bath and shower, central heating, phone, TV, minibar
Facilities extended sitting room, breakfast room, bar, terrace, garden
Credit cards MC, V
Children welcome
Disabled reasonable ground floor access
Pets accepted
Closed 2 weeks Feb
Languages English, Italian
Proprietor Krenberger family

Vienna

Suburban hotel

Gartenhotel Glanzing

This is a rarity – an urban hotel catering for families and for business executives. Just outside the middle of the city in the 'green belt', this address is on a quiet, villa-lined street above the castle and park of Pötzleinsdorf. Romy and Wolfgang Kleemann inherited this 1920's cube-like house and turned it into a hotel. Their own Biedermeier furniture adds character to the drawing room, which also has a piano.

With young children of their own, they understand the needs of families, so the garden provides an informal play area and baby-sitting can be arranged. No wonder this is a favourite with embassy staff awaiting permanent accommodation and also with business people accompanied by their families.

Breakfast is buffet-style with plenty of fresh rolls and home-made jams. This is the only meal served but there are plenty of restaurants in nearby wine villages. In addition, the two suites have kitchen facilities as well as private terraces with stunning views across Vienna towards the UNO city. All guests have free use of the small gym, sauna, and solarium. Public transport into the city is not on the doorstep; getting into the city is easier by car.

Nearby Pötzleinsdorf Park, Heurigen villages.

1190 Wien, Glanzinggasse 23
Tel (0222) 47042720
Fax (0222) 470427214
Location on quiet, villa-lined street, private garage but parking no problem
Meals breakfast, snacks
Prices rooms AS780-1880 with breakfast; children under 16 free in parents' room
Rooms 16 doubles with bath and shower, 4 singles with bath or shower; all have central heating, phone, TV, minibar, hairdrier, radio
Facilities breakfast room, TV room, gym, solarium, garden
Credit Cards DC
Children welcome
Disabled 1 double; lift/elevator from garage
Pets accepted
Closed never
Languages English, French, Italian, Swedish
Proprietor Romy and Wolfgang Kleemann

Vienna

Suburban pension

Hotel Jäger

For over 75 years this has been a family-run enterprise and with Frau Karger's daughter coming into the business, the tradition looks set to continue. Even the resident Vizsla is an hospitable dog. Helene Karger knows exactly what a 'charming small hotel' should be, both as hotelier and as guest, having used our guide to Italy on a recent holiday.

Although Hernalser Hauptstrasse is a main throughfare, the 3-storey villa is set back from the road, with lawn and lime trees providing a buffer. Bedrooms on that side are double-glazed, so noise is not a problem. The lobby features polished wood panelling and a gleaming tiled floor, plus watercolours of 19thC Viennese street scenes. Simplicity is the overall style, though some might call it functional. What makes this bed and breakfast special? The owners, whose welcome is genuine and whose friendliness is natural.

For longer stays, especially with children, the apartment with its own kitchen is ideal; reserve early for school holidays. Tram number 37 stops opposite the entrance and takes about half an hour to get to the city centre.

Nearby Heurigen villages, Kongressbad swimming pool.

1170 Wien, Hernalser Hauptstr 187
Tel (0222) 4641310
Fax (0222) 4666208
Location in quiet suburb of Hernals; ample car parking
Meals breakfast, snacks
Prices rooms AS850-1600 with breakfast; extra bed in room AS300
Rooms 14 double, all with bath or shower; 3 single with shower; 1 suite with kitchen; all have central heating, phone, TV, minibar, hairdrier
Facilities 2 breakfast rooms, TV room, garden, terrace
Credit Cards MC, V
Children welcome
Disabled not suitable
Pets accepted
Closed never
Languages English, French, Italian
Proprietor Helene Karger

Vienna

City hotel

Hotel König von Ungarn

Book well ahead to stay in what many consider the 'jewel in the crown' of Viennese hotels, right in the heart of the old city and only steps away from St Stephen's Cathedral. The present building dates from the 18thC, part of a complex that includes the famous 'Figarohaus' where Mozart composed 'The Marriage of Figaro'.

Sitting in the enclosed courtyard, with wood panelling, etched glass and a tree, you can imagine yourself back in the days of the Austro-Hungarian Empire. Then, the nobility would stay here for months at a time, attending to courtly duties as well as taking in glittering social events. Some of their portraits line the corridors above, whose windowed galleries are an architectural curiosity. Upstairs, the bedrooms are less glamourous, with the sort of comfortable furnishings found in a private house. The restaurant, with chandeliers lighting the vaulted baroque ceiling, has a high reputation for traditional Austrian cuisine. At lunchtime, it is full of businessmen tucking into boiled beef from the trolley.

The polished service and formal atmosphere does not come cheaply but may be worth it for the 'Viennese experience'.
Nearby St Stephen's Cathedral, Fiaker tours.

1010 Wien, Schulerstr 10
Tel (0222) 515840
Fax (0222) 515848
Location central; public underground car parking close by
Meals breakfast; lunch, dinner in restaurant (under separate management)
Prices rooms AS1150-3000 with breakfast
Rooms 21 double with bath or shower; 4 single with shower; 8 suites, all with bath; all have central heating, phone, TV, minibar, hairdrier, radio, air-conditioning
Facilities large atrium courtyard with bar, conference room
Credit Cards DC, MC, V
Children welcome
Disabled some facilities, lift/elevator takes wheelchairs
Pets accepted
Closed never, restaurant Sat
Languages English, French, Italian, Spanish, Portuguese
Manager Peter Valouch

Vienna

City hotel

Hotel Römischer Kaiser Wien

Another romantic hotel with a history, this was built as a baroque mansion in 1684 for Johann Hueber, an Imperial counsellor. Later it became a school for engineering under Maria Theresa. Since 1904, it has been owned by the Jungreuthmayer family who have taken care to maintain the old-world flavour of this listed building.

Chandeliers, arches, mouldings, and gilt work have been preserved with newer furniture carefully chosen to blend in with traditional styles. A parlour, with tapestry-covered chairs, provides a useful meeting place. Bedrooms come in a variety of sizes and shapes; some have modern furnishings in neutral colours, others are so rich with gold, cream and brocade that 1990's push-button telephones and digital clocks look strangely out of place.

Outside, mischievous carved faces look down on locals and visitors taking time off from shopping and sightseeing at the hotel's pavement café. Annagasse is a narrow street just off the fashionable Kärntnerstrasse, between the Opera House and St Stephen's Cathedral. Arriving by car, use the hotel entrance on Krugerstrasse.

Nearby Staatsoper, Stadtpark, Burggarten, museums.

1010 Wien, Annagasse 16
Tel (01) 51277510
Fax (01) 512775113
Location in pedestrian area in heart of city, public car park in Beethovenplatz
Meals breakfast, snacks
Prices rooms AS1600-2600 with breakfast
Rooms 24 double, all with bath and shower, central heating, phone, TV, minibar, hairdrier, radio and air-conditioning

Facilities sitting room, bar
Credit Cards AE, DC, MC, V
Children accepted
Disabled not suitable
Pets not accepted
Closed never
Languages English, French, Italian
Proprietor Dr. Gerhard Jungreuthmayer

Vienna

City hotel

Hotel am Schubertring

No wonder this is a favourite of visiting musicians and artists, who enjoy being on the doorsteps of the Musikverein and the Konzerthaus, with the Staatsoper only a short walk away. Our inspector, an architecture fan, enthuses about the bar, whose mahogany, marble and brass fittings imitate the style of Adolf Loos. Streamlined and rather masculine, this look continues throughout the hotel; there is not a swirling line, frilly curtain, or gilt-edged moulding in sight. Muted colours ranging from cream and peach to blue and brown are easy-on-the-eye. Bedrooms come in all shapes and sizes, as often happens when old buildings are converted, and corridors are long and winding, with sudden turns and changes of level. The staff combines the brisk efficiency of a city hotel with the warmth that attracts families.

Even though it is right on the busy junction of the Ring and Schwarzenbergplatz, rooms are quiet (particularly the suites, each with two bathrooms). Owner Marietta Mühlfellner-Jeannée marks the changing seasons with branches of pussy willow hung with painted eggs at Easter and, of course, a Christmas tree at Yuletide.

Nearby Staatsoper, concert halls.

1010 Wien, Schubertring 11
Tel ((0222) 717020
Fax (0222) 7139966
Location between the opera house and park on the Ring, corner Schwarzenbergplatz; public car parking nearby
Meals breakfast, bar snacks
Prices rooms AS1050-2000 with breakfast; children up to 6 free
Rooms 30 double, 6 single, 3 suites, all with bath and shower; all have central heating, phone, TV, minibar, hairdrier, radio, and air-conditioning
Facilities lobby, bar
Credit Cards AE, MC, V
Children welcome
Disabled 3 rooms with facilities
Pets accepted
Closed never
Languages English, French, Italian, Arabic
Proprietor Marietta Mühlfellner-Jeannée

Vienna

City bed-and-breakfast hotel

Hotel Amadeus

No prizes for guesssing the theme of this hotel. Some find the cherry-red, white and gold of the furnishings excessive, like the over-sweetness of a *Mozartkugel*; others rate it for location, central and equidistant from all the major sites.

■ 1010 Wien, Wildpretmarkt 5 **Tel** (01) 5338738 **Fax** (01) 533873838 **Meals** breakfast **Prices** rooms AS910-1800 with breakfast **Rooms** 29, all with bath or shower, central heating, phone, TV, minibar, radio **Credit Cards** AE, DC, MC, V **Closed** Christmas week **Languages** English, French, Italian

---

Town hotel

Hotel Attaché

The brutally modern exterior belies the friendly ambience of this hotel, where many staff have worked for years. Sleep in a hand-painted wooden bed or under a dramatic canopy. Popular with business visitors (weekdays) and families (weekends).

■ 1040 Wien, Wiedner Hauptstr 71 **Tel** (0222) 5051817 **Fax** (0222) 5051817232 **Meals** breakfast **Prices** rooms AS850-1950 with breakfast; children under 6 free **Rooms** 24 all with bath or shower, central heating, phone, TV, minibar, radio **Credit Cards** AE, DC, MC, V **Closed** never **Languages** English, Italian, Spanish, Portuguese, Polish, Russian, Arabic

---

Town hotel

Hotel Bajazzo

The extrovert new owner, Anne Marie Bogicevic, exemplifies the mix of nationalities in Vienna: her father is Hungarian and she speaks five languages. Practical and modern. Close to old city for sight-seers.

■ 1010 Wien, Esslinggasse 7 **Tel** (0222) 5338904 **Fax** (0222) 5353997 **Meals** breakfast **Prices** rooms AS1180-2480 with breakfast **Rooms** 12, all with bath or shower, central heating, phone, TV, minibar **Credit Cards** MC, V **closed** never **Languages** English, Arabic, Hungarian, Serbo-Croat

---

Near Vienna

For visitors who prefer to stay near the capital, rather than in it, we list the towns where we have recommended hotels within about 80 km/1 hour's drive of Vienna. Some are in Niederösterreich, listed between pages 104 and 122: Baden, Dürnstein, Klein-Wien, Klosterneuburg, Krems, Laaben, Mautern, Mayerling, Payerbach, Puchberg am Schneeberg, Tullnerbach and Weissenkirchen. The rest are in Burgenland, listed between pages 135 and 140: Eisenstadt, Gols, Mörbisch, Neusiedl and Purbach.

Vienna

Suburban villa

Hotel Cottage

In the leafy, up-market residential area of Döbling, this turn-of-the-century villa features huge windows, wrought-iron railings, balconies, and a garden. Favoured by academics visiting the nearby University departments.

■ 1190 Wien, Hasenauerstr 12 **Tel** (0222) 3125710 **Fax** (0222) 31257110 **Meals** breakfast, dinner, snacks **Prices** rooms AS900-1750 with breakfast, children under 10 free; meals from AS120 **Rooms** 22, all with bath or shower, central heating, phone, TV, minibar, radio **Credit Cards** AE, DC, MC, V **Closed** never **Languages** English, French, Italian

---

City pension

Hotel-Pension Elite

'Old-fashioned and proud of it' should be the motto of this unpretentious but well-kept pension. The huge double beds are an unexpected bonus but beware when booking: not all rooms have en suite bathrooms and no credit cards are accepted.

■ 1010 Wien, Wipplingerstr 32 **Tel** (0222) 53325180 **Fax** (0222) 5355753 **Meals** breakfast **Prices** rooms AS540-1400 with breakfast, children under 6 free **Rooms** 27 all with central heating, phone **Credit Cards** not accepted **Closed** never **Languages** English, French, Italian

---

City pension

Hotel-Pension Museum

Another pension that harks back to an earlier era. Furnishings are bland, even dowdy, but some bedrooms are enormous, with views of the High Courts and nearby museums. Popular with visiting professors and art lovers.

■ 1070 Wien, Museumstr 3 **Tel** (0222) 934426 **Fax** (0222) 93442630 **Meals** breakfast, snacks **Prices** rooms AS450-1350 with breakfast; children under 6 free **Rooms** 15, all with bath or shower, central heating, phone, TV **Credit Cards** AE, MC, V **Closed** never **Languages** English, French, Italian, Portuguese

---

City pension

Pension am Operneck

For those on a budget, particularly opera lovers. Recommended by one fan who bought standing tickets and went every night. Simple, straightforward, clean, and small. Breakfast served in the bedrooms.

■ 1010 Wien, Kärntnerstr 47 **Tel** (0222) 5129310 **Meals** breakfast in bedroom **Prices** rooms AS480-825 with breakfast, children under 6 free **Rooms** 6, all with shower, central heating, phone, TV, radio **Credit Cards** not accepted **Closed** 2 weeks Mar **Languages** English, French

Burgenland

Hotels in Burgenland

The easternmost state in Austria is also the least Austrian. Until 1921 it was part of Hungary and life here is almost Mediterranean, lived at a slower pace in warmer weather that produces almonds, figs, apricots and table grapes. But it is grapes for wine that dominate the landscape of the *puszta*, the flat, northern end of the province. The southern end is wooded, hilly and flecked with castles.

Perhaps the most famous local inhabitants are the storks that nest on the thatched rooftops near the Neusiedl lake, which attracts vast numbers of birds and birdwatchers to the reed beds that ring this unusually warm and shallow inland sea. The lake is also a playground for holidaymakers who take advantage of the constant breezes to wind-surf and sail.

Accommodation is simpler and certainly cheaper than elsewhere in Austria, ranging from modern seaside-style boxes to rooms in old castles. Because the weather is milder and holidaymakers come primarily in the summer, furnishings are more basic.

There are also the *Buschenschenken*, taverns owned by wine-producers to show off the quality of their vineyards. Many have gipsy-style music, as much for tradition as tourism in the area that produced Liszt. Music is in the blood here, with Eisenstadt a popular destination during the annual Haydn Festival in September. Roast goose and red cabbage is the traditional fare on St Martin's Day (November 11) which is celebrated all over Austria, but particularly in Burgenland.

In Eisenstadt, the state capital, the Parkhotel is a useful spot in the middle of town (Tel (02682) 4361, 28 rooms), as is the Hotel Eder (Tel (02682) 2645, 25 rooms); both are family-run.

Golf fans head for either the Landhaus Römerstein (Tel (03154) 6290, 20 rooms) or Sporthotel Harry Krainz (Tel (03154) 6266, fax 626690, rooms 35) in Jennersdorf.

We would welcome reports on a revamped hotel in Rust, one of the most charming villages on the western shore of Neusiedl lake complete with Renaissance and baroque houses. The Hotel and Restaurant Sifkovits (Tel (02685) 276, fax 36012, 30 rooms) is a mixture of old and new. The new is all glass and concrete which makes it rather cool. Perhaps it needs time for the Tomschitz family to develop its character.

For further details about the area contact:
Landesfremdenverkehrsverband für das Burgenland,
Schloss Esterhazy,
A-7000 Eisenstadt.
Tel (02682) 3384.
Fax (02682) 338420.

This page acts as an introduction to the features and hotels of Burgenland and gives brief recommendations of good hotels that for one reason or another have not made a full entry. The long entries for this state — covering the hotels we are most enthusiastic about — start on the next page. But do not neglect the shorter entries starting on page 140; these are all hotels that we would happily stay at.

Burgenland

Castle hotel, Bernstein

Burg Bernstein

What do you expect from a castle? This one not only has towers and fortifications, it has a dungeon complete with whipping bench, rack, and cells plus an armoury and an 'Alchemist's Kitchen'. The public can see all this, plus the former Knights' Hall. This is now a restaurant and boasts a splendid early 17thC stuccoed ceiling by Bartolomao Bianco, portraying scenes from Greek mythology. Concerts are held here from time to time. The rest of the castle is for hotel guests.

They enjoy the sitting-rooms, one with ancestral portraits and a lovely baroque tiled *Kachelofen*, another with a huge open fireplace. Even the staircase excites art buffs: it is believed to be designed by Fischer von Erlach, the greatest of Viennese baroque architects. As for bedrooms, each is different but all are furnished with antiques and are virtually suites. The atmosphere is of yesteryear: no phones, no televisions, no minibars. On cool evenings, wood-burning stoves provide whatever warmth is needed. Some bathrooms are decidedly old-fashioned but these are in some of the most popular rooms, so guests obviously take it all as part of the experience.

Nearby castles; riding; Bucklige Welt.

7434 Bernstein **Tel** (03354) 6382 **Fax** (03354) 6520 **Location** in wooded hills above village; car parking in courtyard **Meals** breakfast, dinner, snacks **Prices** rooms AS620-1500 with breakfast; DB&B from AS770; reductions for children **Rooms** 10 double, 1 single; all have bath	**Facilities** dining-room, 2 sitting-rooms, bar; terrace, outdoor swimming-pool; sauna **Credit Cards** AE, MC, V **Children** welcome **Disabled** access to ground floor bedroom **Pets** accepted **Closed** Nov to 1 May **Languages** English, French, Italian **Managers** Berger family

Burgenland

Gasthof Edith Gibiser

Steeply-roofed, thatched cottages are a feature of the flat countryside down here on the Hungarian border, and Edith Gibiser has cleverly incorporated the style into her hotel, or rather her 'hotel complex'.

The Gasthof itself is a solid, square, stone inn complete with terrace dotted with red parasols. Here, the restaurant has a reputation for authentic Pannonian dishes, which have a Hungarian influence. *Zigeuner Fleisch* (a mixture of chicken, beef and pork in a paprika sauce) and herb strudel are specialities.

It is the area behind the inn, however, that captivated our inspector. In the lush meadow that climbs the hillside are new, thatched bungalows that children love to stay in. Each looks like a fairy-tale cabin where Little Red Riding Hood or Snow White would feel at home.

Inside are solid, bright pine beds, tables and chairs with pretty curtains and an individual *Kachelofen*. Parents appreciate the comfort and the modern bathrooms, as well as TV and covered porches for sun-bathing. A nearby *Biotop*, or pond, occupies city children for hours, studying the wildlife.

Nearby Güssing mineral water museum; Schlösslberg; cycling.

7561 Heiligenkreuz im Lafnitztal, Hauptstr 81
Tel (03325) 216
Fax (03325) 24644
Location on Hungarian border; ample car parking
Meals breakfast, lunch, dinner, snacks
Prices rooms AS450-1200 with breakfast; DB&B from AS550; reductions for children; meals from AS110
Rooms 20 double; all have bath or shower, central heating, phone, TV, minibar
Facilities 3 dining-rooms, bar; terrace
Credit Cards DC, MC
Children accepted
Disabled not suitable
Pets accepted
Closed 2 weeks Christmas; Feb
Languages English, French, Italian, Hungarian
Proprietor Edith Gibiser

Burgenland

Holiday hotel, Mörbisch

Hotel Restaurant Schmidt

Appearances can be deceptive. From the main street of this pleasant, lakeside village with medieval church towers, Das Schmidt looks like just another well-built house. Behind, however, is a modern extension with two tiers of arcades looking on to a large terrace with yellow and white sunshades. Right at the top are the 'Storks' nests'. These four suites are decorated in soft blue and beige, with maple and cherry-finished furniture crafted by a local carpenter. Large enough for families, they are also suitable for the disabled, with specially fitted bathrooms. The lift/elevator ensures access. The Schmidt family deserve a commendation for their efforts; this is one of the few hotels we have found that takes this provision seriously.

Elsewhere, the furnishings look a little old-fashioned, mainly in shades of brown or, in the restaurant, red and green. Modern stained glass is a feature; one series of panels represents the four seasons, another has landscape and village scenes from Burgenland. All rooms have views of the lake and there is a play area for children plus a large garden. Herr Schmidt makes his own wine; try his speciality, *Welschriesling*.

Nearby lake, beach; open-air theatre; vineyards.

7072 Mörbisch am See, Hauptstr 71
Tel (02685) 8294
Fax (02685) 829413
Location on main street; own car parking spaces
Meals breakfast, lunch, dinner, snacks
Prices rooms AS460-1300 with breakfast; DB&B from AS560; reduction for children; meals from AS80
Rooms 21 double, 2 single, 4 suites; all have bath or shower, central heating, phone; TV on request
Facilities 2 dining-rooms, sitting-room, bar, TV room; terrace; indoor swimming-pool, health spa
Credit Cards not accepted
Children very welcome
Disabled 4 bedrooms
Pets accepted
Closed Nov to Easter
Languages English, French, Italian
Proprietors Schmidt family

Burgenland

Gasthof Seewirt

As we have emphasized in the introduction, Burgenland offers simpler accommodation than other parts of Austria. Walter and Marianne Karner have expanded their holiday hotel on the eastern edge of the Neusiedl lake, which has echoes of sea-side Greece or Spain. The Seewirt Hotel has a new annexe, the Haus Attila and it is here that our inspector feels that familes will have an enjoyable holiday. 'The lake view on a hazy day is quite stunning, with sailing boats and windsurfers flickering over the water'. Lawns and poplar trees surround the buildings which have developed from the simple peasant house pictured on the entrance hall wall, dating from 1924.

The third generation of Karners demolished that in 1979 and put up the square, ordinary Seewirt, followed more recently by the Attila. 'Make sure you book into the Attila' is our inspector's advice. The Seewirt is brown and neutral; the Attila snowy-white, with new pine furniture and much more room for the blue and white easy chairs and sofas. The food is Pannonian, reflecting the quasi-Hungarian cuisine using local carp, zander and eel, accompanied by Herr Karner's own wines.

Nearby lake, bathing; stork's nests; vineyards.

7141 Podersdorf am See
Tel (02177) 2415
Fax (02177) 246530
Location on lake shore; own car parking
Meals breakfast, lunch, dinner, snacks
Prices rooms AS350-1000 with breakfast; DB&B from AS450; reductions for children; meals from AS100
Rooms 21 double in Haus Attila; all have bath or shower, central heating, phone, TV, radio
Facilities dining-room, sitting-room, TV room; terrace; sauna
Credit Cards not accepted
Children very welcome
Disabled access to bedrooms; lift/elevator
Pets not accepted
Closed Nov to Feb
Languages English, French, Hungarian
Proprietors Karner family

Burgenland

Restaurant with rooms, Purbach

Weingut Am Spitz

Despite its undistinguished, modern bedrooms, our inspector was still impressed by the spectacular setting, the history and design of the restaurant and the genuine charm of the Schwarz family.

Am Spitz has its own vineyards, and the Friday evening meals, complete with a dozen wines, are a great attaction for gourmet weekenders. Down below are the monks' baroque cellars, complete with huge barrels and wine-tasting facilities. The estates' Welschriesling, Sauvignon Blanc and Blaufränkisch are of particularly high quality. The 70-year old restaurant is in what was once the gatehouse of the monastery and is unusually eye-catching, with a voluted baroque façade. All around are lawns studded with chestnut trees, oleanders and ancient stone walls, which make a fine backdrop for summer dining.

Because this is all so attractive, the simple, modern bedrooms in a separate building beyond the car park are a little disappointing. However, the beds are comfortable, bathrooms practical and prices reasonable so our inspector would happily sleep off a fine meal here. Two bedrooms are specially adapted for wheelchair users.

Nearby Purbach; lake; cycling, hiking.

7083 Purbach, Waldsiedlung 2
Tel (02683) 5519
Fax (02683) 551920
Location on hill above town; ample car-parking
Meals breakfast, lunch, dinner
Prices rooms AS400-800 with breakfast; DB&B from AS550; reductions for children; meals from AS250
Rooms 11 double, 1 suite; all have shower, central heating, phone; TV on request
Facilities 5 dining-rooms, sitting-room, bar, TV room; terrace, garden
Credit Cards not accepted
Children welcome
Disabled easy access; 2 adapted bedrooms
Pets accepted
Closed Christmas to Easter
Languages English, French, Hungarian, Czech
Proprietors Schwarz family

Burgenland

Restaurant with rooms, Eisenstadt

Gasthof-Restaurant Ohr

Johannes Ohr's cooking has made a name for this simple hotel. Austrians flock to enjoy dishes based on asparagus in May, strawberries in June, mushrooms in August and goose in November. Useful stop when touring Burgenland.

■ 7000 Eisenstadt, Rusterstr 51 **Tel** (02682) 2460 **Fax** (02682) 4481 **Meals** breakfast, lunch, dinner **Prices** rooms AS420-1320 with breakfast; meals from AS120 **Rooms** 25, all with bath or shower, TV **Credit Cards** not accepted **Closed** Mon **Languages** some English

---

Restaurant with rooms, Gols

Hotel Birkenhof

A useful stop-over on the way to visit the sights of western Hungary. Enjoy a meal with Helmut Beck's own wines; attentive service, friendly staff. The building is modern and undistinguished. Sunny terrace. Wine-tastings in cellar.

■ 7122 Gols, Festwiese 14 **Tel** (02173) 2346 **Fax** (02173) 242520 **Meals** breakfast, lunch, dinner, snacks **Prices** rooms AS 320-780 with breakfast; meals from AS80 **Rooms** 21, all with bath or shower, central heating, phone, radio; TV on request **Credit cards** DC, MC, V **Closed** one month after Ash Wed **Languages** English, French

---

Castle hotel, Lockenhaus

Burg Lockenhaus

Make sure you reserve a room in the 800-year old castle itself, rather than the modern annexe. Behind the towering walls and red-and-yellow shutters are a medieval courtyard, Renaissance stairway, and echoing bedrooms with antique furniture.

■ 7442 Lockenhaus **Tel** (02616) 2394 **Meals** breakfast, lunch, dinner, snacks **Prices** rooms AS590-700 with breakfast; meals from AS100 **Rooms** 7 in castle, 27 in annexe, all with bath or shower, central heating, phone **Credit cards** not accepted **Closed** never **Languages** English

---

Town hotel, Neusiedl am See

Hotel Leiner

Strictly for bird-watchers, who flock here from all over Europe to spot rare varieties on the Neusiedler Lake. The cheerful welcome offered by Franz and Andrea Leiner makes up for the modest rooms, near the station. Hearty meals.

■ 7100 Neusiedl am See **Tel** (02167) 2489 **Fax** (02167) 2907 **Meals** breakfast, dinner, snacks **Prices** rooms AS320-640 with breakfast; meals from AS100 **Rooms** 10, all with bath or shower, central heating, phone, TV **Credit cards** not accepted **Closed** never **Languages** English, Hungarian

Kärnten

Hotels in Carinthia

Carinthia is Austria's own Riviera, with the massive Tauern range of mountains protecting the southernmost Federal State from the worst extremes of the weather. A belt of picturesque lakes, running from east to west, provides that Mediterranean feeling, often decorated with resort hotels and promenades. The biggest and most famous is the Wörthersee where the water can reach 28°C in summer. High standards of cleanliness are observed, so swimming is just as popular as sailing, wind-surfing and boating. Petrol-engines are banned in favour of electric power. In winter, Carinthia is just as popular, blessed with the sunny, southern slopes of the Tauern as well as the Karawanken range on the Italian and Slovenian borders. As the region has long been a national, as well as an international, playground, the standard of hotel-keeping and restaurants is particularly high.

Bad Kleinkirchheim is a fine example of the quality of the region. Small, family-run hotels with a high reputation include the Berghof (Tel (04240) 468, fax 479, 16 rooms); Hinteregger (Tel (04240) 477, fax 4777, 18 rooms) and Schneeweiss (Tel (04240) 401, fax 813052, 29 rooms).

Across in the Nockberge National Park, Eisentratten is a pleasant base, with the Gasthof Lindenhof known for its traditional cooking (Tel (04732) 2780, fax 312822, 30 rooms).

Just outside the popular lakeside resort of Pörtschach on the Wörthersee lake is the Seehotel Schorn with its own garden and beach. (Tel (04272) 2277, fax 227750, 35 rooms).

Gmünd is a pilgrimage town for car-worshippers as Ferry Porsche was born here. Apart from the Porsche Museum, Gmünd itself, with its old walls, is worth exploring. The Gasthof Kohlmayr is on the main square (Tel (04732) 2149, fax 2153, 24 rooms).

For many Austrians, the Drautal is the prettiest in the province. Little disturbs the peace of a small town like Lendorf, so families enjoy holidays at hotels like the Gasthof Oswald (Tel (04769) 2430, fax 243040, 34 rooms).

The Weissensee lake is the highest in Carinthia, where swimming is popular. Frozen in winter, it is a favourite with the Dutch to engage in their national sport. The Haus am See is right on the water, and very sports-orientated (Tel (04713) 2222, 20 rooms).

For further details about the area, contact:
Kärntner Tourismus Gesellschaft m.b.H.,
Halleggerstr 1,
A-9201 Krumpendorf.
Tel: (04229) 2224.
Fax: (04229) 2089.

This page acts as an introduction to the features and hotels of Carinthia and gives brief recommendations of good hotels that for one reason or another have not made a full entry. The long entries for this state – covering the hotels we are most enthusiastic about – start on the next page. But do not neglect the shorter entries starting on page 157: these are all hotels that we would happily stay at.

Kärnten

Hotel Kapeller

This is the place for golfers, skiers, walkers, and families. There is a practice golf hole behind the hotel with a putting green and sandtraps; the 18-hole course is nearby in Bad Kleinkirchheim. Skiers head across the snow to the Nockalm Cable Car in the morning and ski back in the afternoon. Hiking trails abound and as for families, the owners have small children of their own, so the more the merrier. Inside, the layout is open-plan, with no precious, breakable objects; outside there are swings, slides, and a hillside to play on.

Bedrooms are furnished in brown but lightened by large windows. There are long bureaus for books, cameras and so on, large wardrobes for sports clothes and deep balconies for privacy. Bathrooms are similarly well-laid out.

Downstairs, everyone congregates around the open fire or in the new, pale wood-pannelled bar. Overall, the hotel is practical and comfortable; the charm is provided by Ingeborg Fritzer, whose young staff are lively, friendly yet always professional. The chef, for example, has to be inventive, since regulars book in for up to 5 weeks.

Nearby winter sports; golf, walking trails; thermal baths

9546 Bad Kleinkirchheim, St.
Oswald 72
Tel (04240) 482
Fax (04240) 48340
Location on hillside, above
St. Oswald; ample car parking
Meals breakfast, lunch,
dinner, snacks
Prices DB&B AS610-1700 for
2; reduction for children
Rooms 16 double, 2 single, 2
suites; all have bath or shower,
central heating, phone, TV,
hairdrier

Facilities 2 dining-rooms, 2
sitting-rooms, bar, TV room,
games room, terrace; sauna,
little children's room
Credit Cards AE, DC
Children very welcome
Disabled not suitable
Pets accepted
Closed mid-Oct to mid-Dec;
mid-April to mid-May
Languages English, French,
some Italian
Proprietors Dickermann-
Fritzer family

Kärnten

❊ **Resort hotel, Bad Kleinkirchheim** ❊

Hotel Römerbad

Ingrid Putz was an early convert to the benefits of whole-food and organic products. Not only are the breakfast breads baked each morning, the grains are ground just before mixing. "At first my staff and even my family were incredulous"; then they saw, and tasted, the difference." Dried fruits, honey, and fruit juices provide sweetness instead of sugar, and only a minimum of butter is used. Our inspector is wary of many whole-food meals but even he was won over by the elegant presentation and delicious flavours. Anyone inspired by these methods can learn the techniques in special classes and take away recipes for use at home. Of course, 'normal' menus are also on offer; there is no pressure to change one's diet.

Similarly, you can do absolutely nothing at all, even though health and fitness are the themes of this hotel. A wide variety of treatments are available and the Kaiserberg ski-lift and Römer thermal baths are only minutes away. Set high on a south-facing hillside, the hotel is open and spacious, with a rather sophisticated ambience. Bedrooms are well-furnished, most have a balcony and there are special *Bio* bedrooms.

Nearby thermal baths; winter sports; hiking, golf, tennis.

9546 Bad Kleinkirchheim
Tel (04240) 84540
Fax (04240) 823457
Location on hill above main road through village; ample car parking
Meals breakfast, lunch, dinner, snacks
Prices AS680-1380 with breakfast; DB&B from AS740; reductions for children; meals from AS200
Rooms 24 double, 4 single; all have bath or shower, central heating, phone; most have TV
Facilities 2 dining-rooms, sitting-room, bar, TV room; terrace, fitness and health spa
Credit Cards AE, DC, MC
Children very welcome
Disabled not suitable
Pets accepted
Closed 21 April to 21 May
Languages English, Italian
Proprietors Putz family

Kärnten

Kleines Hotel Kärnten

'To create a hotel to match the view' was the aim of the Tschemernjak family. 'The view' is a panorama across Faaker See to the Mittagskogel rising above other mountains. No wonder when they started as just a bed-and-breakfast in 1972 guests wanted them to serve other meals. "They just didn't want to leave."

Now they stay put and enjoy, for example, hand-made ravioli, leeks from the garden, and lamb with thyme sauce; wines come from small producers, unavailable in the shops. Luise Tschemernjak is in the kitchen, her son is the sommelier, while her husband does everything else. They are locals with extended families: cheese comes from one cousin, another is a butcher.

The hotel is unashamedly modern, with rooms decorated in soft grey and suites in yellow, green, rose or blue. The dining-room, sitting-room, and corridors all boast original works of art, many by a German who came as a child and is now a well-known painter. There are hiking trails and watersports but many guests, our inspector included, prefer to relax in the garden under the cherry trees, admiring that spectacular view.

Nearby Faaker See

9580 Egg am Faaker See, Egger Seepromenade 8
Tel (04254) 2375
Fax (04254) 237523
Location in meadows above lake; ample car parking
Meals breakfast, lunch, dinner, snacks
Prices rooms AS800-2700 with breakfast; DB&B from AS1860 for 2
Rooms 12 double, 4 suites; all have bath or shower, central heating, phone, TV, hairdrier, radio, safe; minibar in suites
Facilities dining-room, sitting-room, terrace; garden, own dock and beach
Credit Cards not accepted
Children welcome
Disabled not suitable
Pets not accepted
Closed Nov to Easter
Languages English, French, Italian
Proprietors Tschemernjak family

Kärnten

Old guest-house, Faakersee

Gasthof Tschebull

How do you make a Carinthian feel homesick? Just mention Tschebull, a small hotel with a big restaurant on the edge of the Faaker See. Always open and always busy, this could be written off as just a popular road-side beer-garden and terrace. That would be a mistake. Hans and Willi Tschemernjak are serious chefs, serving up what they call *'Alpeadria'* cooking: a regional style that transcends the nearby borders of Italy and Slovenia.

In the old *Lobiserstub'n*, decorated with Switbert Lobiser wood-cuts, our inspectors ordered home-smoked eel with home-made rolls, duck breasts with corn dumplings and roast lamb with rosemary gravy, finishing off the meal with walnut ice-cream and hot spice cake with chocolate sauce. Hans' son Johannes runs the hotel and by 1993 aims to complete the renovation and expansion programme that will make the quality of the lodging equal to the food. Room 108 is an example of the new high standard: pale wood, thick moss-green carpets and a little sun-room. The bath-room is sumptuous, with glass, brass and pale pink marble plus double wash-basins and a jacuzzi. Our only quibble is over the breakfast: plastic-wrapped butter and jam seem out of place.
Nearby lake, woods, hiking.

9580 Egg am Faakersee, Egger Seeuferstr 26
Tel (04254) 2191
Fax (04254) 219137
Location on road, near lake; ample car parking
Meals breakfast, lunch, dinner, snacks
Prices rooms AS400-1050 with breakfast; reductions for children; meals from AS150
Rooms 13 double, 1 suite; all have bath or shower, central heating, phone, TV, radio

Facilities 3 dining-rooms, terrace, garden
Credit Cards DC
Children very welcome
Disabled access to all rooms
Pets accepted
Closed never; restaurant 2 weeks Jan
Languages English, French, Italian
Proprietors Tschemernjak family

Kärnten

Island hotel, Faakersee

Inselhotel

Half the fun is getting there. Park next to the the shore, use the special phone and minutes later, a sleek launch slips into the landing stage. This is the transport to the small island, no more than 100m wide and 800m long, that sits in the middle of one of Austria's loveliest lakes; and it all belongs to the Inselhotel.

You can go out just for the day but for the full experience, stay the night. The hotel is some 50 years old, with small dark sitting areas around the reception desk plus a large, square dining room and terrace overlooking the water. Upstairs, corridors are cool and wide; bedrooms are plain, with views of the lake through chestnut trees. Bathrooms tend to be white and clinical. Like lodges in American national parks, the look is dated, but who cares? Guests pad about in shorts and bare feet; they play tennis, use the boats, or walk in the woods. Children beg permission to stay the night in the Villa Muh, an old barn near the main building. A nanny keeps small ones amused in July-August. Shore excursions are simple, since the boatman is on duty 24 hours a day. As if on cue, a fawn raced out of the woods and across the lawns just as our inspector was leaving.

Nearby lake, tennis, woods.

9583 Faakersee, Faak am See
Tel (04254) 2145
Fax (04254) 214577
Location on a small island in middle of lake; ample car parking by ferry boat-house; telephone for collection
Meals breakfast, lunch, dinner, snacks
Prices DB&B AS570-2400; reductions for children; meals from AS200
Rooms 10 suites, 17 double, 5 single; all have bath or shower, phone, radio, safe; TV on request
Facilities dining-room, sitting-room, bar, 2 terraces, TV room, games-rooms; tennis-courts, sailing boats, gardens
Credit Cards not accepted
Children very welcome
Disabled not suitable
Pets accepted, on lead
Closed mid-Oct to mid-May
Languages English, Italian
Proprietor Bucher and Catasta families

Kärnten

✳ **Country inn, Feld am See** ✳

Hotel Lindenhof

Set beside a splashing fountain and a church, the Lindenhof is at the heart of the quiet lakeside village of Feld am See. Locals still drink in the *Stube* with its pale wood, bright turquoise seats and deep window sills, crammed with old coffee pots and dolls. Outsiders flock to the 'modern rustic' dining rooms for award-winning cooking. When our inspectors visited, the menu offered broccoli and artichoke terrine, trout cooked with Noilly Prat, steak in a red wine sauce and a rich chocolate terrine.

Comfortable armchairs abound downstairs. Upstairs, the bedrooms in the older building are rather dull, but the newer 'studios', refurbished and expanded in 1990, have extra sitting space, terraces, modern carved country furniture, hyacinth-blue curtains, and bathrooms with lots of shelf space. However, most of them overlook the cemetery.

The Nindlers, whose family have been here for over a century, are always making improvements, such as the sparkling new fitness room in the basement with the latest technology, as well as special low-calorie menus. Cross country enthusiasts ski around the lake, but the nearest downhill is at Bad Kleinkirchheim. **Nearby** lake, tennis; winter sports.

9544, Feld am See
Tel (04246) 2274
Fax (04246) 227450
Location in centre of village; car parking outside
Meals breakfast, lunch, dinner, snacks
Prices rooms AS360-1200 with breakfast; DB&B from AS460; reduction for children; meals from AS120
Rooms 21 double, 4 single, 2 suites; all have bath or shower, central heating, phone, radio; TV by request **Facilities** 2 dinning-rooms, 3 sitting-rooms, bar, TV room, terrace; beauty and health farm, own lakeside beach with games
Credit Cards AE, DC, MC (restaurant only) **Children** very welcome **Disabled** not suitable **Pets** accepted **Closed** mid-Nov to mid-Dec; 3 weeks Jan; after Easter **Languages** English, French, some Italian **Proprietors** Hermann and Monika Nindler

Kärnten

Wayside inn, Grosskirchheim

Nationalparkhotel Schlosswirt

You need time to get the best out of this wayside inn on the famous Grossglockner road. Hubert Sauper has immersed himself in local history and knows all the national park's secret beauty spots. With the help of his wife and family, he renovated the little castle behind the hotel and filled the stables with sure-footed Haflingers. "Dishing up *Schnitzels* and beer is easy on this road. I look for a challenge." So he retraced the steps of the 19thC wine-traders, complete with authentic costume. Now guests can follow part of the same route, go riding, hunting and fishing, or merely admire the wildlife and flowers.

The busy road is quiet when the high pass is closed at night and throughout the winter. The old *Stuben* have the obligatory horns on the walls, but hay-filled cushions and pink tablecloths, too. The food is honest, regional cooking with soup, sausage and cheese always available. The cheerful bedrooms have plain, solid furniture (made in the village) brightened by cheerful prints. Special events include wine-tastings, Sunday evening dinner in the medieval *Schlössl*, or a torch-lit sleigh-ride.

Nearby local museum; Grossglockner; winter sports, national park.

9843 Grosskirchheim-Döllach
Tel (04825) 211
Fax (04825) 211165
Location on southern side of Grossglockner High Pass; car parking outside hotel
Meals breakfast, lunch, dinner, snacks
Prices rooms AS490-1620 with breakfast; DB&B from 580; reduction for children; meals from AS100
Rooms 24 double, 4 single; all have bath or shower, central heating, phone; TV on request
Facilities 3 dining-rooms, bar, TV room; terrace, sauna, tennis courts, stables
Credit Cards not accepted
Children very welcome
Disabled not suitable
Pets accepted
Closed usually Nov
Languages English, French, Italian
Proprietors Hubert and Maria Sauper

Kärnten

❊ **Mountain hotel, Heiligenblut** ❊

Haus Senger

Not many sports stars have turned to hotel-keeping as successfully as Hans Senger, who represented Austria at the 1952 Olympic Games. His small hotel, wedged into a steep hill above Heiligenblut, is a careful mixture of old and new. Rebuilt in 1966, it looks like an old farmhouse thanks to the 400-year old beams and planks rescued from an old barn. These, along with the stone-flagged floors and crackling open hearth, give the dining-room and *Stube* the atmosphere holidaymakers dream about.

Upstairs, most bedrooms are interlinked so they can be used individually or as suites, with connecting doors soundproofed by mattresses. All are decorated in country style with fabrics of soft red, blue or green. Some suites have kitchenettes so parents can make breakfast while the children run around in pyjamas. The *Romantik Zimmer* boasts a four-poster bed painted blue and hung with white muslin curtains.

Menus range from Italian and French dishes to the regular Wednesday fondue evenings. A new wing, with a health and fitness area, blends in cleverly and guests ski out and ski back from a side door. A hotel that is better in reality than in its brochure.

Nearby Grossglockner, winter sports, hiking.

9844 Heiligenblut
Tel (04824) 2215
Fax (04824) 22159
Location up sharp turn off main road above village; ample car parking
Meals breakfast, dinner, snacks
Prices rooms AS450-1600 with breakfast; DB&B from AS550-890; reductions for children
Rooms 3 double, 2 single, 8 suites; all have bath or shower,
central heating, phone, TV, radio **Facilities** dining-room, 3 sitting-rooms, bar, TV room; table-tennis room, gymnasium, sauna, solarium, children's room
Credit Cards not accepted
Children very welcome
Disabled not suitable **Pets** accepted **Closed** Oct to mid-Dec; after Easter to mid-June
Languages English, French, Italian **Proprietors** Senger family

Kärnten

City hotel, Klagenfurt

Romantikhotel Musil

Sightseers in Klagenfurt's old quarter photograph the Dragon Fountain, the Trinity Column, and the Old and New Town Halls. Those in the know then head for the Musil *Konditorei*. Open every day of the week, it is always busy, with customers queuing for cakes and pastries, plus a dozen sorts of ice-cream. Most of all, however, they ask for chocolates because in this part of Austria, Musil means chocolate.

The *Konditorei* is part of the elaborately-decorated hotel that has been in the Musil family since 1926. The look throughout is pure 19thC. Take a light meal in the inner courtyard, more elegant than any modern atrium. Ornate lights, wrought-iron railings, and a skylight 3 floors up provide a setting worthy of ladies in long skirts and hats. The tiny *Stub'n*, full of old guns and trophies from local hunters, serves up smoked salmon mousse, venison cutlets with cranberry sauce and sweetcorn dumplings. Each bedroom is different, but all have a romantic look. You may find a sleigh-bed, a huge gilt mirror, parquet floors, or flowery wallpaper; bathrooms, however, are new with all the conveniences of a luxury hotel.

Nearby old town; Europapark; Minimundus.

9020 Klagenfurt, 10 Oktoberstr 14
Tel (0463) 511660
Fax (0463) 516765
Location in middle of city; public car parking, 4 garage spaces
Meals breakfast, lunch, dinner, snacks
Prices rooms AS1200-2500 with breakfast; reductions for children; meals from AS250
Rooms 11 double, 1 single; all have bath or shower, central heating, phone, TV, air-conditioning, minibar, hairdrier, safe
Facilities 2 dining-rooms, sitting-room, bar
Credit Cards AE, DC, MC, V
Children welcome
Disabled reasonable access, with lift/elevator
Pets accepted
Closed Dec 25, Jan 1
Languages English, some French, Italian
Proprietors Musil Family

Kärnten

❋ **Town hotel, Kötschach-Mauthen** ❋

Hotel Post

Every Austrian town has a 'Post' hotel. Some are old and full of character, others are more like barracks with high ceilings and echoing corridors. Here, Margit Klauss shows what taste and imagination can do. Her husband, Wilfried, heads the adventure holiday programme of ski-touring, river-rafting, trekking and fishing which are all carefully graded for age and ability.

Everything is large, from the dining-room with its arched windows overlooking the main street of Kötschach to the children's room with its playhouse and stock of toys. New paint and curtains throughout in 1992 have given a fresh look to all the public rooms. Bedrooms vary: number 14 is a converted attic with dormer windows looking into tree-tops; number 108 has a parquet floor, a sitting area, and a view of the church. The beds are in a variety of woods and styles. In the new annexe, chairs and curtains are in matching fabrics and bathrooms are small but adequate. Suites here even have cooking facilities. Between the old and new buildings is a garden with a heated swimming-pool and fish-pond; the connecting passageway underground leads past a comprehensive health and fitness area.

Nearby local ski area, winter sports, mountains.

9640 Kötschach-Mauthen
Tel (04715) 2210
Fax (04715) 22253
Location in middle of village opposite church; ample car parking behind and under cover
Meals breakfast, lunch, dinner, snacks
Prices rooms DB&B AS630-1820; reductions for children; meals from AS150
Rooms 21 double, 6 suites; all have bath or shower, central heating, phone, TV, radio; many with hairdrier
Facilities 2 dining-rooms, sitting-room, bar, TV room, games room, 2 terraces; large sauna and health area, heated outdoor swimming-pool, children's room **Credit Cards** MC, V **Children** very welcome
Disabled not suitable **Pets** accepted **Closed** Nov
Languages English, French, Italian **Proprietors** Klauss family

Kärnten

Sissy Sonnleitner's Kellerwand

Sissy Sonnleitner is a star, voted Austria's 'Chef of the Year' in 1990. Yet she does not work in Vienna, Salzburg, or even a posh ski-resort, but in the village of Mauthen. Find it on the River Gail, a few minutes' drive from the Italian border. Apart from inspiration derived from family holidays in France and Germany, she is self-taught. Her repertoire combines Carinthian and Friuli dishes: she fills pasta Austrian-style, with white cheese, potatoes and herbs but stuffs dumplings Italian-style, with pumpkin.

Kurt Sonnleitner's wine-cellar scores for its competitive prices and wide range of vintages from Italy, Bordeaux, Burgundy and Austria. Breakfast is served under the arches in the peaceful courtyard. The 500-year old *Kellerwand,* with yellow walls and blue shutters, is the oldest building in Mauthen and has been in the family for 90 years. A half-way house for travellers between Venice and Vienna, it merits more than an overnight stay. Those who settle in for a month on half-board are never offered the same dish twice. Bedrooms match the high standards of the cooking: Thonet furniture and Ralph Lauren fabrics with Carrara marble in the bathrooms.

Nearby alpine and cross-country skiing; fishing, rafting.

9640 Kötschach-Mauthen
Tel (04715) 269
Fax (04715) 37816
Location in middle of village; ample car parking
Meals breakfast, lunch, dinner, snacks
Prices rooms AS420-1250 with breakfast; DB&B from AS545; children under 6 free in parents' room; meals from AS385 (gourmet menu)
Rooms 5 double, 5 suites, 2 apartments; all have bath or shower, central heating, phone, TV, minibar
Facilities dining-room, sitting-room, library, bar; terrace, garden
Credit Cards AE, DC, MC, V
Children very welcome
Disabled not suitable
Pets accepted
Closed mid-Nov to mid-Dec; 1 week after Easter
Languages English, Italian
Proprietors Sonnleitner family

Kärnten

Lakeside villa, Ossiachersee

Hotel Dreimäderlhaus

The village of St. Andrä is at the southern end of the Ossiachersee, Carinthia's third largest lake. Here the mountains drop down dramatically to the water. Locals consider it barely warm enough for swimming, even in high summer, although hardy visitors jump right in.

Just 100 m from the St. Andrä ferry landing stands this secluded holiday villa. Built 60 years ago by the current owner's grandparents, bedrooms retain the style of the 1930s, with white-painted beds and cane headboards, free-standing wardrobes, and high ceilings. Each has a private bathing cabin on the shore, reached by a walkway through bullrushes. There is also a dock, plus swings and table-tennis for children. Adults sit on the terrace, looking across the lake towards Annenheim. Pleasant at breakfast, it is dramatic in the evening, when floodlights illuminate the huge *Fichten* (spruce trees) framing the view. At the back is a 'mountain hut' complete with red-checked tablecloths, a hunting horn, and open fire. We would be more enthusiastic about this guest-house if the interior were freshened up; although open just four months a year, standards must be maintained.

Nearby lake, water-sports; hiking.

9523 Landskron/Villach, St. Andrä, Ossiachersee
Tel (04242) 41227
Location in park on edge of lake; ample car parking
Meals breakfast, snacks
Prices AS290-1040 with breakfast; reductions for children
Rooms 10 double, 3 single, 2 suites; all have bath or shower, phone
Facilities breakfast-room, bar; terrace

Credit Cards not accepted
Children very welcome
Disabled not suitable
Pets accepted
Closed Oct to May
Languages English, French, some Italian
Proprietors Strafinger family

Kärnten

❋ **Lakeside hotel, Weissensee** ❋

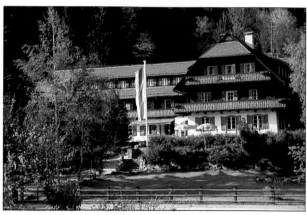

See-und Gartenhotel Enzian

The Weissensee, Carinthia's highest lake, provides year-round sport. In winter, skaters and cross-country skiers whizz across the snow and ice; in summer, it is warm enough for swimming and all the other water sports. On a dead end road is the Enzian, a delightful bed-and-breakfast set in a flower-filled garden. It has a tennis court, dock and lakeside lawn, even a sailing and windsurfing school.

Recently renovated, it was built by Herr Cieslar's parents, and heirlooms such as clocks, a wedding veil, and photographs add character. More is provided by Beatrix Mayr-Hassler, the energetic manageress.

The *enzian* (gentian) theme appears in carvings on shutters and in the blue of tablecloths in the breakfast-room. Inviting armchairs and good reading lamps give the sitting-room the look of a private house, while the recently-renovated bedrooms are medium-sized, mainly with white walls and floral curtains. Where the rest of the hotel is light and airy, the *Almhütte,* just outside, is dark, cosy and perfect for an après-ski or late evening schnapps. Dinner is taken at the sister hotel next door.

Nearby Weissensee, winter sports

9762 Techendorf am Weissensee
Tel (04713) 2221
Fax (04713) 2305
Location on hillside above lake; ample car parking
Meals breakfast, snacks; lunch, dinner at nearby Ferienhotel
Prices AS500-2000 with breakfast
Rooms 4 single with shared bath or shower; one single, 16 double, 3 suites all with bath or shower; all have central heating, phone, TV,
Facilities sitting-room, terrace; garden, tennis court, boats; use of pool, sauna next door
Credit Cards not accepted
Children welcome
Disabled not suitable
Pets accepted
Closed mid-Oct to mid-Dec; mid-March to mid-May
Languages some English, Italian
Proprietors Cieslar family

Kärnten

Castle hotel, Wörthersee

Burg Drasing

Peter and Renate Heinzl fell in love with this 900-year old stronghold in February 1987 when it was dusted with snow. Now these Viennese *restaurateurs* run it as a delightfully informal holiday retreat, high above Krumpendorf, tucked into thick woods on a narrow country lane.

The black gate with its foot-long key looks forbidding on arrival. Once inside the imperial-yellow walls, however, the atmosphere is more cheerful. Arched balconies surround the central courtyard. Sunny, the dog, has his own tartan rug on the stone-slab floor. Suits of armour stand to attention next to antique chests, cupboards and boxes of logs in the medieval corridors. The dining-room and bar are equally imposing. All four bedrooms are vast, some floored with foot-wide planks. Number 1 has windows looking south and west 'where you can watch storms roll in from Italy on hot summer nights'. The Biedermeier furniture is complemented by modern bedside tables; curtains are long, in pale grey and rose satin. Sleeping, walking and eating are the main activities for the mainly professional people who have discovered this haven.

Nearby lake, woods, hiking, riding, tennis.

9201 Krumpendorf,
Drasingerstr
Tel (04229) 2160
Fax (04229) 2635
Location on hillside,
overlooking lake; car parking
outside
Meals breakfast, dinner,
snacks
Prices rooms AS1100-2200
with breakfast
Rooms 4 double; all have bath
or shower, central heating,
phone, TV

Facilities dining-room, sitting-room, billiard room; terrace,
outdoor swimming-pool
Credit Cards not accepted
Children accepted
Disabled not suitable
Pets accepted
Closed Oct to mid-Dec; Jan to
mid-June
Languages English
Proprietors Heinzl family

Kärnten

Castle hotel, Wörthersee

Schloss Hallegg

"The best place in the world to have breakfast." That was the reaction of our inspector who, like all first-time visitors, was open-mouthed at the view. Where else in the world can you sip coffee and munch rolls outdoors on top of castle ramparts? Far below, the land drops away sharply and in the distance, beyond the trees and fields, are the twin towers of Maria Saal.

The castle is approaching its 800th birthday. Built on a rocky outcrop, it is large enough to garrison a small army. Enter the huge portal and you expect to see knights in armour. Instead, roses fill the courtyard and old-fashioned sleds and carriages shelter in the cloisters. Two more stories of arches climb to the steep wood-shingled roof. Everything is on a huge scale, with high ceilings and wood floors. Bedrooms could sleep whole families, while the medieval hall could be a film set. Forty metres long, 9 metres high, with vicious-looking weapons on the wall, it cannot look much different than it did when Otto II of Hallegg lived here. Open only in summer, guests walk in the woods, fish on the private lake, play tennis, and peep into the tiny chapel in the tower, big enough for only 2 pews.

Nearby lake, tennis, woods, fishing, riding.

9201 Krumpendorf am Wörthersee, Halleggerstr 131
Tel (0463) 49311
Location in woods, high above Krumpendorf; ample car parking
Meals breakfast
Prices AS500-1100 with breakfast; reductions for children
Rooms 15 double; all have bath or shower, phone, minibar; TV by request
Facilities dining-room, sitting-room, tennis-court
Credit Cards not accepted
Children very welcome
Disabled not suitable
Pets accepted
Closed Oct to mid-May
Languages some English
Proprietor Frau Melita Helmigk

Kärnten

❋   Mountain hotel, Afritz   ❋

Hotel Lärchenhof

The Tronigger family is sports-mad as the array of trophies shows. Families spend time on the 3 tennis courts, in the swimming-pool and hiking. In winter, they ski straight from the door. Public rooms and bedrooms are plain.

■ 9542 Afritz-Verditz **Tel** (04247) 2134 **Fax** (04247) 213411 **Meals** breakfast, lunch, dinner, snacks **Prices** DB&B AS380-840 **Rooms** 23, all with shower, central heating, phone **Credit cards** not accepted **Closed** Oct to mid-Dec; after Easter to early May **Languages** English

❋   Mountain resort hotel, Bad Kleinkirchheim   ❋

Hotel Kaiserburg

Tucked between private houses on the Kaiserburg side of the main road, the ski lifts are virtually at the door, the thermal baths just a 5-minute walk. Indoor pool overlooks garden. A jolly ambience thanks to the Hermann family.

■ 9546 Bad Kleinkirchheim **Tel** (04240) 365 **Fax** (04240) 3658 **Meals** breakfast, lunch, dinner, snacks **Prices** rooms AS440-1350 with breakfast; meals from AS120 **Rooms** 27, all with bath or shower, central heating, phone **Credit cards** not accepted **Closed** Nov to mid-Dec; short period after Easter **Languages** English, Italian

❋   Village hotel, Bad Kleinkirchheim   ❋

Hotel Sonnalm

Quiet location at the end of the village and just a stone's throw from lift connections to the Nockalm and Maibrunn- Kaiserburg systems. Modern, above average comfort. Huge picture windows in the spacious sitting and dining rooms. Large garden.

■ 9546 Bad Kleinkirchheim **Tel** (04240) 507 **Fax** (04240) 8505 **Meals** breakfast, lunch, dinner, snacks **Prices** DB&B AS650-1750 **Rooms** 24, all with bath or shower, central heating, phone, TV, radio **Credit cards** not accepted **Closed** April (depending on Easter); Nov to mid-Dec **Languages** English, Italian, some French

Farmhouse hotel, Diex

Berggasthof Jesch

Tucked into the south-eastern corner of Carinthia, Diex is one of the sunniest villages in Austria. The Jesch family farm provides horse-riding as well as fresh produce for the table. Suitable for children. Rural simplicity.

■ 9103 Diex, Wandelitzen 10 **Tel** (04232) 7196 **Meals** breakfast, lunch, dinner, snacks **Prices** rooms AS230-500 with breakfast; meals from AS100 **Rooms** 22, all with bath or shower, central heating, phone, TV **Credit cards** not accepted **Closed** Nov to April **Languages** English

Kärnten

Country inn, Faaker See

Bernold's Landhotel 'Gasthof Post'

Old-fashioned and rather dark inside but brightened by the enthusiasm of Herr Bernold, who has expanded his hotel into a mini-empire with restaurant, nightclub, bistro, tennis courts and private beach nearby. Also owns Villa Faakersee across the street.

■ 9580 Drobollach am Faaker See, Seeblickstr 47 **Tel** (04254) 2184 **Meals** breakfast, lunch, dinner, snacks **Prices** rooms AS300-900 with breakfast; meals from AS120 **Rooms** 30, all with bath or shower, central heating, phone, TV, radio, minibar, safe **Credit cards** AE, DC **Closed** never **Languages** English

---

✻　　Mountain guest-house, Feld am See　　✻

Gasthof-Pension Hubmannhof

Quiet location on hillside with view of Feld am See and valley. In summer, chickens scratch for food, hay dries in the meadow, and guests take the sun on the terrace, walk and enjoy watersports. Simple, clean and inexpensive.

■ 9544 Feld am See, Wiesen 8 **Tel** (04246) 2667 **Meals** breakfast, dinner, snacks **Prices** rooms DB&B AS275-750 **Rooms** 10, most with bath or shower, central heating **Credit cards** not accepted **Closed** never **Languages** English

---

Town hotel, Friesach

Friesacherhof

Friesach, with its moat and old walls, is Carinthia's oldest town and well worth exploring. Alfred Pötscher's simple hotel is on the ancient main square near the famous fountain. Rooms at the front have a splendid view, but lack sound-proofing.

■ 9360 Friesach, Hauptplatz 4 **Tel** (04268) 2123 **Meals** breakfast, lunch, dinner, snacks **Prices** rooms AS180-600 with breakfast; meals from AS110 **Rooms** 15, all with bath or shower, central heating, phone, TV **Credit cards** AE, DC, MC, V **Closed** never **Languages** English

---

✻　　Wayside inn, Grosskirchheim　　✻

Hotel Post

At the southern end of the Grossglockner Pass, in the heart of the Hohe Tauern National Park, Franz-Josef Sauper's yellow-painted hotel is popular with hikers in summer. Skiers go to Heiligenblut in winter. Pleasant garden; modern health spa.

■ 9843 Grosskirchheim **Tel** (04825) 205 **Fax** (04825) 20519 **Meals** breakfast, lunch, dinner, snacks **Prices** rooms AS260-760 with breakfast; meals from AS80 **Rooms** 28, all with bath or shower, central heating, phone, TV **Credit cards** AE, DC, V **Closed** 2 weeks after Easter **Languages** English

Kärnten

Country hotel, Ledenitzen

Restaurant-Pension Forellenhof

A jolly, family and sports-oriented hotel with huge swimming-pool and tennis courts near Faakersee. Big breakfasts and hearty dinners are chef Helmut Kerschbaumer's specialties. Try the trout and venison, then indulge in home-made cakes.

■ 9581 Ledenitzen, St. Martinstr 16 **Tel** (04254) 2371 **Fax** (04254) 4078 **Meals** breakfast, lunch, dinner **Prices** rooms AS 320-700 with breakfast; meals from AS150 **Rooms** 28, all with bath or shower **Credit Cards** AE **Closed** Mon (Oct-Apr); Jan, Feb **Languages** some English, some Italian

Lakeside hotel, Millstatt am See

Hotel Hubertusschlössl am See

Only a lawn separates this 19thC house, with romantic tower, from the Millstättersee. Choose Room 24 for its balcony and summertime view of boats and windsurfers. The Hohenwarter-Sodek family also own the modern Hotel Seewirt nearby.

■ 9872 Millstatt am See, Kaiser-Franz-Josef-Str **Tel** (04766) 2110 **Fax** (04766) 211054 **Meals** breakfast; lunch, dinner at Hotel Seewirt **Prices** rooms AS400-1620 with breakfast; meals from AS120 **Rooms** 19, all with bath or shower, central heating, phone, TV, minibar, radio **Credit cards** AE, DC, MC, V **Closed** Oct-Apr **Languages** English, French, Italian

Health farm, Millstättersee

Biohotel Alpenrose

The Obweger's inn is recognized as Austria's first Biohotel, setting the trend for organic food, health-conscious diets and rooms furbished in natural materials like wood and cotton. Overlooks Millstättersee lake. Outdoor swimming-pool.

■ 9872, Millstatt am See, Obermillstatt 84 **Tel** (04766) 2500 **Fax** (04766) 3425 **Meals** breakfast, lunch, dinner, snacks **Prices** rooms DB&B from AS900 for 2 **Rooms** 27, all with bath or shower, central heating, phone, TV **Credit cards** not accepted **Closed** first 2 weeks Dec; last 2 weeks Jan **Languages** English

Guesthouse, Ossiach

Gasthof-Pension Schlosswirt

Plain, unpretentious and inexpensive, this is popular because of its lively young staff. Sit outside under gold and white striped umbrellas and order coffee and home-made cakes. Some rooms have a lake view and the private dock is 3 minutes away.

■ 9570 Ossiach 5 **Tel** (04243) 347 **Meals** breakfast, lunch, dinner, snacks **Prices** rooms AS320-760 with breakfast; meals from AS 100 **Rooms** 6, all with bath or shower, central heating, phone **Credit cards** not accepted **Closed** Nov to April **Languages** English, Italian

Kärnten

Village inn, Paternion

Gasthof Tell

A useful overnight halt to experience a jolly 700-year old inn in the Drau valley. The enthusiasm of the Michorl family makes up for the old-fashioned furnishings. Carinthian dishes are a speciality in the busy *Stube*. Dancing in the cellar-bar.

■ 9711 Paternion **Tel** (04245) 2931 **Fax** (04245) 3026 **Meals** breakfast, lunch, dinner, snacks **Prices** rooms AS250-300 with breakfast; meals from AS100 **Rooms** 18, all with bath or shower, central heating, phone, TV **Credit cards** AE, DC, MC, V **Closed** never **Languages** English

---

Restaurant with rooms, Ruden

Gasthof Pfau Obstgut

Eat, sleep and wander round the orchards where some of Austria's most famous *Schnaps* is made. Franz Lamprecht's restaurant enjoys a burgeoning reputation. Renovated bedrooms in the century-old building, more in a new extension.

■ 9113 Ruden, Untermitterdorf 1 **Tel** (04234) 8221 **Fax** (04234) 8220 **Meals** breakfast, lunch, dinner **Prices** rooms AS220-500 with breakfast; meals AS85 **Rooms** 7, all with bath or shower, central heating, phone, TV **Credit cards** not accepted **Closed** Jan to March; restaurant only Mon, Tues in April, Oct-Dec **Languages** English

---

Town hotel, St Veit an der Glan

Hotel Mosser

St Veit is such an historic town that it deserves better accommodation. In a quiet side street, the Mosser has plain bedrooms above a modern bar and restaurant. Adequate as a base to explore the medieval squares and fortifications.

■ 9300 St Veit/Glan, Spitalgasse 6 **Tel** (04212) 3223 **Fax** (04212) 322210 **Meals** breakfast, lunch, dinner, snacks **Prices** rooms AS270-540 with breakfast; meals from AS100 **Rooms** 15, all with bath or shower, central heating, phone, TV **Credit cards** not accepted **Closed** never **Languages** English

---

Lakeside hotel, Wörthersee

La Promenade

One to watch. Parisian chef Ervé Delclos and his Austrian wife, Ulrike, opened this quiet hotel 4 years ago. They deliberately omit both phone and TV from the bedrooms, so guests really can relax. Classic French sauces in the restaurant.

■ 9201 Krumpendorf am Wörthersee, Strandpromenade 5 **Tel** (04229) 2763 **Fax** (04229) 3784 **Meals** breakfast, lunch, dinner, snacks **Prices** rooms AS350-1350 with breakfast; meals from AS150 **Rooms** 15, all with bath or shower, central heating **Credit cards** AE, MC, V **Closed** mid-Oct to end Nov; 2 weeks end Jan **Languages** English, French

Kärnten

Lakeside hotel, Wörthersee

Hotel Solaris

This hotel scores for location: a few steps from the Krumpendorf boat stop and private beach, near tennis courts and surrounded by parkland. The large, covered terrace is a bonus but despite a 1990 renovation, furnishings are bland, though comfortable.
■ 9201 Krumpendorf am Wörthersee, Wieningerallee 35 **Tel** (04229) 2818 **Fax** (04229) 281842 **Meals** breakfast, lunch, dinner, snacks **Prices** DB&B AS610-1400 **Rooms** 26, all with bath or shower, central heating, phone, TV in suites **Credit Cards** MC, V **Closed** mid-Oct to mid-May **Languages** English, French, Italian

---

Lakeside villa, Wörthersee

Villa Riva

Right on the water, with statues on the lawn, the former summer home of King Alfonso XIII of Spain remains both luxurious and exclusive. Apartments only, and furnished like a private house. Most guests in high season stay a minimum of 2 weeks.
■ 9210 Pörtschach, Wörthersee, Hauptstr 293 **Tel** (0472) 32100 **Fax** (0472) 321747 **Meals** breakfast, lunch **Prices** rooms AS1200-4000, with breakfast **Rooms** 16, all with bath, shower, central heating, phone, TV, minibar, kitchenette **Credit cards** AE, DC, MC, V **Closed** Oct to April **Languages** English, French, Italian

---

Lakeside villa, Pörtschach am Wörthersee

Seehotel Frech

Although Dr Claudia Brugger has converted her parents' elegant summer-house into a bed-and-breakfast, it still looks and feels like a private home. Right on the water, with its own dock; protected from the road by a large garden.
■ 9210 Pörtschach am Wörthersee, Töschling 80 **Tel** (04272) 2447 **Meals** breakfast **Prices** rooms AS1000-1650 with breakfast **Rooms** 6, all with bath or shower, phone, TV **Credit cards** not accepted **Closed** Oct to April **Languages** English

---

Lakeside hotel, Velden am Wörthersee

Seehotel Tropic

The Wenger family want everyone to have fun at this attractive hotel that is the width of a lawn away from the water. The lakeside café, dock and boats are all part of their 'Beach Club' that attracts younger visitors.
■ 9220 Velden, Klagenfurterstr 40 **Tel** (04274) 2037 **Fax** (04274) 203742 **Meals** breakfast, lunch, dinner, snacks **Prices** rooms AS480-2100 with breakfast; meals from AS110 **Rooms** 14, all with bath or shower, central heating, phone, TV, radio, minibar, safe **Credit cards** not accepted **Closed** never **Languages** English, French

Steiermark

Hotels in Styria

Styria advertises itself as the 'Green Heart of Austria' and certainly has miles of unspoilt countryside. As the second-largest state, it also has large variations of landscape, ranging from the Totes Gebirge, the Dead Mountains in the north-west, to the flat plains in the east; rolling hills in the south are covered in vineyards, whilst the Dachstein range is a skier's and climber's delight.

Small, family-run hotels abound for holiday-makers. In the mountains of the north-west, Ramsau sits on a plateau above Schladming. Two of the best hotels are the Alpenkrone, run by Albert Pilz (Tel (03687) 81414, 12 rooms), open all year for hiking and cross-country skiing, and Karl Wieser's Hotel Berghof (Tel (03687) 81848, 33 rooms).

Down in Schladming itself, the Romantik Hotel Alte Post is over 350 years old, and there is a mixture of furnishings both old and new which can jar a little. But all is forgiven at the dining-table where the Huber family are famous for their carefully-prepared Styrian dishes (Tel (03687) 22571, fax 225718, 40 rooms).

Schladming grew on the wealth produced from local copper and silver mines, but today it is skiing that is the great draw. A popular base, just outside the town, is the Hutegger family's Gasthof Berghof (Tel (03687) 61396, fax 6114713, 12 rooms).

Also high in the mountains at Haus im Ennstal is the Hotel Hauser Kaibling, highly sports-oriented with impressive facilities from an indoor pool to an outdoor tennis court (Tel (03686) 2378, fax 237850, 27 rooms).

Bad Aussee is both a health spa and a ski resort in the Traun valley. Modern, but still traditional in style, is the Alpenhof (Tel (06152) 2777, 10 rooms). The Gasthaus Staud'nwirt is a simple, friendly place for an overnight stay (Tel (06152) 2427, 15 rooms).

Elsewhere, the Lindenhof at Auffen is a square, country inn with authentic local dishes (Tel (03333) 2320, 10 rooms). More unusual is the Familien Ballonhotel at Hofkirchen (Tel (03334) 2262, fax 226221, 18 rooms) which specializes in small children... and ballooning.

Another specialist hotel is the Tennishotel Enzianhof, some 30 km southwest of Graz (Tel (03143) 2106, fax 210641, 30 rooms). The brick-red courts are the main attraction.

For further details about the area contact:
Steiermark Werbung,
Herrengasse 16,
8010 Graz.
Tel (0316) 4030330.
Fax (0316) 40303310.

This page acts as an introduction to the features and hotels of Styria and gives brief recommendations of good hotels that for one reason or another have not made a full entry. The long entries for this state – covering the hotels we are most enthusiastic about – start on the next page. But do not neglect the shorter entries starting on page 178: these are all hotels that we would happily stay at.

Steiermark

❋ **Converted hunting lodge, Altaussee** ❋

Hubertushof

'One of a kind' was our inspector's reaction, after a tour with the owner, Countess Strasoldo-Graffenberg. Most Austrian inns have a few hunting trophies on the wall; here there are hundreds, in the entrance hall, above the stairs and in the corridors. Many pre-date the house, built in 1894 for the Countess's grandparents. The atmosphere of yesteryear remains, but without the gloom of some old buildings. It still looks and feels like a private home where guests are invited, rather than paying, to stay. In the sitting-room, a grandfather clock ticks loudly opposite an open fire; a hand-written note on the desk announces that the bar is open from 5.30-7pm.

'Enchanting' was the comment on the terrace's picture-postcard vista of the lake, plus the Loser and Trisselwand mountains. Above is the private balcony of the suite, 'one of the prettiest I've ever seen' and dazzlingly white with highlights of blue. Room four, a total contrast, is a bold combination of royal blue and cherry red; number three has painted country furniture. The hospitality extends to details: a box of tissues, a shoe horn and a nail file set out on a table, a lap-rug on a *chaise longue*.

Nearby Altaussee lake; Loser cable-car; winter sports.

8992 Altaussee, Puchen 86
Tel (06152) 71280
Location on hillside above village; ample car parking
Meals breakfast
Prices AS580-1500 with breakfast
Rooms 7 double, 2 single, 1 suite; all have bath or shower, central heating, phone; some TV
Facilities breakfast room, sitting-room, bar; terrace, garden

Credit Cards AE, DC, MC, V
Children welcome
Disabled not suitable
Pets accepted
Closed mid-Oct to 26 Dec; 11 Jan to 1 Feb; March, April, May; open at Easter
Languages English, some French, Italian
Proprietor Countess Rosemarie Strasoldo-Graffenberg

Steiermark

❄ **Lakeside hotel, Altaussee** ❄

Hotel Seevilla

This resort was a favourite of composers and writers in the 19thC. Arthur Schnitzler and Gustav Mahler visited; so did Brahms, whose Piano Trio in C Major, Opus 87 and Spring Quintet in F Major, Opus 88, were played for the first time in a house on this site. Not much has changed; lilacs still bloom in spring while the birch and ash, chestnut and maple trees shade the lakeside walk from summer sun. Ducks waddle to the water, plunge in and swim out towards the moored sailboats. At the far end of this small lake, granite cliffs drop right down to the clear water. Our inspector lunched on the terrace, sampling Styrian sour cream soup, and cured ham served on a wooden platter.

Built in l980, the Seevilla stands among summer homes where the road ends at the lake. Modern comforts are combined with traditional style; carved wood is everywhere. Elaborate wrought-iron is used for wall-lights, radiator covers, and railings up the marble spiral staircase. Otherwise, furnishings are unexceptional and the conservative shades of brown, green, and dull red make rooms rather dark. Bedrooms are plain, though each one has a balcony.

Nearby lake, tennis, hiking, fishing; winter-sports.

8992 Altaussee
Tel (06152) 71302
Fax (06152) 7130282
Location at end of lane on lake; ample car parking
Meals breakfast, lunch, dinner, snacks
Prices rooms AS500-1150 with breakfast; DB&B from AS875; reductions for children; meals from AS150
Rooms 27 double, 3 single; all have bath or shower, central heating, phone, TV, minibar, radio
Facilities 2 dining-rooms, sitting-room; terrace, sauna
Credit Cards AE, DC
Children welcome
Disabled reasonable access; lift/elevator
Pets accepted
Closed Nov
Languages some English, French, Russian
Proprietors Maislinger-Gulewicz family

Steiermark

❈ **Country hotel, Etmissl** ❈

Etmissler Hof

'From the balcony, you can watch the moon rise twice, on either side of the Hochschwab' wrote our inspector on his visit to this wayside inn. Find it at the end of the road in the hamlet of Etmissl, which itself is at the end of a peaceful valley where pine forests cover rolling hills. The hotel dates from 1788; the Wöls family took over in the 19thC.

Anna Wöls is the sort of owner who is keen for all her guests to enjoy their stay. During the main holiday season there is a daily programme of supervised children's activities, ranging from tractor rides to evening campfires. There is table-tennis, an outdoor, heated swimming-pool, plus a separate building where young-sters can make as much noise as they like. They can play safely in the surrounding meadows, help the chef cook spaghetti and then congregate at their own table for dinner. No wonder it is a well-known member of Austria's children's hotels group: parents can sit back, relax and recharge their own batteries while the younger generation happily wear down theirs. This is popular with people from the UNO city in Vienna who want the outdoor life (skiing and hunting) but plenty of creature comforts.

Nearby hiking; winter sports; Grünersee; Mariazell church.

8622 Etmissl
Tel (03861) 8110
Location at end of lovely valley; ample car parking
Meals breakfast, lunch, dinner, snacks
Prices AS310-1000 with breakfast; DB&B from AS400; reductions for children; meals from AS80
Rooms 25 double, 5 single; all have bath or shower, central heating, phone, radio, minibar; TV on request

Facilities 3 dining-rooms, 2 sitting-rooms, reading-room, bar, 2 TV rooms, table-tennis; 2 terraces, gymnasium, health spa, outdoor swimming-pool, garden
Credit Cards not accepted
Children very welcome
Disabled not suitable
Pets accepted
Closed 10 to 25 Jan
Languages English, French
Proprietors Wöls family

Steiermark

Town inn, Feldbach

Landgasthof Herbst

Johann Herbst is the fourth generation of the family to run this wayside inn in the heart of Styria. The pink-painted, rather modern-looking hotel is through a medieval gateway with a big garden behind, crammed with fruit trees and children's climbing frames. Completely renovated in 1988, the interior has a cool, fresh feel throughout, mostly in spruce wood which shows the grain, or elegant cherry-wood. The older rooms have oak furniture, cream walls and pink or beige materials.

All this is merely a backdrop for the enthusiastic Herbst family whose restaurant is renowned for its Styrian specialities, which range from smoked ham and meat strudel to trout and 'gentleman's goulash'. They will even provide an 'English breakfast' with eggs for visitors feeling home-sick.

The clientele includes businessmen during the week; otherwise, families with small children enjoy the safety of the garden as well as the indoor swimming-pool at the town's leisure centre 200 metres away. 'All in all, a very professionally-run place', says our inspector.

Nearby fortifications, pumpkin-seed oil museum; Schloss Kornberg; cycling, hiking.

8330 Feldbach, Gniebing 15
Tel (03152) 2741
Fax (03152) 274130
Location on main road, just outside town; car parking outside
Meals breakfast, lunch, dinner, snacks
Prices rooms AS480-1100 with breakfast; DB&B from AS590; reductions for children; meals from AS200
Rooms 17 double, 5 single, 1 suite; all have bath or shower, central heating, phone, TV
Facilities 4 dining-rooms, 2 sitting-rooms, bar, table-tennis room; 2 terraces, garden; sauna
Credit Cards AE, DC, MC, V
Children very welcome
Disabled easy access, 3 bedrooms adapted **Pets** accepted; not in restaurant
Closed 22 Dec to 15 Jan
Languages English, French, Italian
Proprietors Herbst family

Steiermark

Town hotel, Graz

Schlossberg Hotel

We include this hotel despite the fact that it has well over 30 bedrooms. Our roving reporter, who has long had a love affair with Graz, was insistent: 'We must include somewhere nice to stay in Graz; this is extraordinarily elegant and it does maintain the charming, small ambience we want'.

Vivid blue, with black shutters, this amalgamation of two 15thC bourgeois houses could not be better placed. Step off the embankment and back in time. The hotel's entrance hall retains its stout pillars and vaulted ceiling. Everywhere antique furniture maintains the sense of history, thanks to Frau Marko's excellent taste, acquired as an antiques dealer. A gilded sconce, like an arm, holds two candles near the reception desk.

Under the exposed beams, a cuddly, cross-eyed gilded lion's head greets visitors who, like our inspector, covet the genuine Biedermeier settee. The only blemish is the bar area, where the modern, leather furniture is somewhat garish. The bedrooms, however, are carefully furnished, often with whitewashed walls and even more antiques. There is a roof-garden with views over the Styrian capital.

Nearby Schlossbergbahn, cathedral; Weapons Museum.

8010 Graz, Kaiser-Franz-Josef-Kai 30
Tel (0316) 80700
Fax (0316) 8070160
Location on river, below Schlossberg; private car parking nearby
Meals breakfast
Prices rooms AS1250-2000 with breakfast; reductions for children
Rooms 27 double, 14 single, 4 suites; all have bath or shower, central heating, phone, TV, minibar, radio
Facilities sitting-room, bar; terrace, outdoor swimming-pool; gymnasium, sauna
Credit Cards AE, DC, MC, V
Children welcome
Disabled 1 bedroom suitable
Pets accepted
Closed never
Languages English, French, Italian
Proprietors Marko family
Manageress Frau Schmidt

Steiermark

Landhaus St. Georg

"I'm just a *Häusl* (jack of all trades)," says Kurt Langs, his keen blue eyes alight with self-mockery. Not only does he change light-bulbs, he built this hotel himself. After 27 years with Austrian Railways, he decided to change career. That was in 1973, when this was just an empty hillside. Two years later, he and his wife opened their inn, with only 4 rooms. Since then, gradual expansion has resulted in first-rate comforts and a clever blending of old and new wood. Here is proof that 'modern' need not mean characterless squares and rectangles.

Take the *Georgstub'n*. A circular table fits neatly into the large bay window, whose shape is echoed by the octagonal bar. Deep red Persian carpets and green tapestry cushions provide colour against a background of knotty pine. Bedrooms are generously-sized and named for the mountain in view, such as Freispitz and Freienstein. Despite the plush furnishings, no eyebrows are raised when hikers return with boots and backpacks. That is because Herr Langs is also a mountain climber, with 200 peaks over 2000 m to his credit. In winter, a beginners' slope and ski-school are only 600 m away.

Nearby Stoderzinken mountain; winter sports; hiking, climbing.

8962 Gröbming 555
Tel (03685) 22740
Fax (03685) 2274040
Location on quiet hillside above private road; ample car parking
Meals breakfast, dinner, snacks
Prices DB&B AS600-1100; reductions for children
Rooms 10 double, 12 suites, 1 single; all have bath and shower, central heating, phone, safe; TV on request

Facilities 2 dining-rooms, bar; conference room, indoor swimming-pool, sauna, steambaths; terraces, garden
Credit Cards AE, DC, MC, V
Children very welcome
Disabled limited access
Pets accepted; not in dining-room
Closed 15 Oct to 15 Dec
Languages English, French, some Italian
Proprietors Langs family

Steiermark

Castle hotel, Kapfenstein

Schlosswirt Kapfenstein

A steep road leads to this small castle that dates from the 11thC. Its hilltop position provided early warning of invading Turks and insurgent Hungarians centuries ago; nowadays, the view across rolling hills into Hungary and Slovenia is peaceful, with vineyards rather than armies marching in regular rows. The only guard to the former fortress is an amiable St. Bernard dog. The style is 'pleasant and comfortable rather than designer-deluxe'; nevertheless, our inspector gave a high rating for the personal atmosphere. Martin and Elisabeth Winkler-Hermaden have run the hotel for over 20 years, establishing a reputation for hospitality that is matched by the quality of their wines.

On the 11 hectares (27 acres) of vineyards in south-west Styria, they grow ten types of grapes, including traditional Austrian varieties such as Ruländer, Blauburger and Blauer Zweigelt. They have also experimented with Sauvignon Blanc, which in 1991 sold out immediately. The barrels, made from local oak, are stored in the 17thC *Löwenkeller*. As for food, the motto is 'light, creative and Styrian', featuring game in the autumn, lamb in the spring, and herbs and vegetables from their own garden.

Nearby Schloss Riegersburg, Schloss Kornberg.

8353 Kapfenstein
Tel (03157) 2202
Fax (03157) 2322
Location on peak of Kapfensteinerkogel; ample car parking
Meals breakfast, lunch, dinner, snacks
Prices rooms AS1000-2000 with breakfast; DB&B from AS1300; reductions for children; meals from AS300
Rooms 6 double; all have bath or shower, central heating, phone, TV
Facilities 2 dining-rooms, sitting-room, TV room; 3 terraces
Credit Cards not accepted
Children very welcome
Disabled not suitable
Pets accepted
Closed Christmas, Feb
Languages English
Proprietors Winkler-Hermaden family

Steiermark

Vineyard hotel, Kitzeck

Weinhof Kappel

'The dignified demeanour of Herr Kappel bespeaks a man who is serious about his business and serious about his wine'. Our reporter was mightily impressed by this stylish modern hotel once he had calmed his nerves after driving up 'a terrifyingly steep, winding hill', on a particularly wet and misty day. Kitzeck, near the Slovenian border, boasts that it is the highest wine-growing region in Europe (560 m) and it was the vineyard that brought Gunther Kappel here in the first place, some 20 years ago. The ancient wine-cellar, complete with splendidly carved and gilded casks, houses his pride and joy, especially the Welschriesling, the Muscatel and Morillon (or Chardonnay). The food is enterprising; a speciality is stuffed chicken breast in a Riesling sauce.

Blue and white sunshades dot the leafy terrace outside; honey-coloured wood and pink tablecloths lend a comfortable yet formal air to the dining-room which has enviable vistas over the vineyards. Just as much care has been taken over the bedrooms which are bigger than average, often with balconies, and have pale pine panelling, floor-length curtains and pots of flowers. **Nearby** vineyard.

8442 Kitzeck, Steinriegel 25
Tel (03456) 2347
Fax (03456) 234730
Location on hilltop among vines; ample car parking
Meals breakfast, lunch, dinner, snacks
Prices rooms AS330-1000 with breakfast; DB&B from AS480; reductions for children; meals from AS200
Rooms 15 double, 1 single; all have bath or shower, central heating, phone, TV, radio

Facilities 2 dining-rooms, sitting-room, TV room; terrace
Credit Cards not accepted
Children welcome
Disabled not suitable
Pets not accepted
Closed Jan, Feb
Languages English
Proprietors Kappel family

Steiermark

❋ **Rural hotel, Pruggern** ❋

Farmreiterhof

'Forget every tired cliché about alpine hotels and alpine vistas. This is the real thing.' Deep in the countryside, the only morning sound our inspector heard was the tinkling of cowbells in the pasture below the house. From his balcony, he watched deer scuttling from the garden into the pine forest.

No wonder he felt envious of the regulars who come here year after year to ski in winter and hike or climb the mountains in summer. The house dates from 1872 and has been in the family for five generations. The Gerharters are natural innkeepers, making little separation between their life and that of the guests. Heinrich teaches in the Federal Forestry and Agricultural School and also edits a local newspaper in Enns. Elisabeth runs the hotel with the help of the granny and the next generation is being primed to take over. The cooking is home-style and filling, with dishes such as *Kasnockerln* (cheese noodles) and *Ennstaler Krapfen* (doughnuts filled with brown crumbly cheese) which are best partnered by *Schnaps*. Peaks such as Grimming, Kammspitze and Dachstein provide names for the bedrooms which, like the rest of the hotel, have rustic, homely comforts.

Nearby winter sports; hiking, riding.

8965 Pruggern 65
Tel (03685) 22692
Fax (03685) 2333377
Location high above village; own car parking
Meals breakfast, dinner, snacks
Prices rooms AS280-560 with breakfast; DB&B from AS380; reductions for children
Rooms 5 double; all have bath or shower, central heating, TV
Facilities dining-room, TV- and sitting-room; terrace; outdoor heated swimming-pool; sauna
Credit Cards not accepted
Children very welcome
Disabled not suitable
Pets not accepted
Closed Christmas
Languages English, some French
Proprietors Gerharter family

Steiermark

Peter Rosegger

A display of mountain-climbing equipment by the front door gives a clue to the favourite summer-time activity at this chalet-style inn, set on a plateau beneath the Dachstein ridge. Fritz Walcher is a well-known mountain guide and runs courses in climbing, starting with children as young as four years old and continuing to advanced level. There is also hiking and year-round skiing on the Dachstein glacier.

As for the name, "we did not want another 'Dachsteinblick' or 'Alpenrose', so chose the famous Styrian romantic poet." Pictures relating to his life hang on the walls, while villages with a Rosegger connection provide names of bedrooms. All have a little entrance hall and large cupboards, while the family rooms at ground level have doors leading into the garden, so children (and pets) can go straight outside. The food is renowned; expect home-smoked trout, yoghurt and goat cheeses from local farms, and teas made from mountain herbs. Organic produce, vegetarian dishes and even flour-free recipes are all served up in the cosy dining-rooms where guests congregate for dinner.

Nearby Dachstein Tauern mountains; winter sports; hiking, climbing.

8972 Ramsau am Dachstein 233
Tel (03687) 81223
Fax (03687) 812238
Location on high plateau; approach via Kulm, follow signs to Vorberg; ample car-parking
Meals breakfast, lunch, dinner, snacks
Prices DB&B AS660-1460; reductions for children
Rooms 6 double, 2 single, 5 family; all have central heating; some have phone
Facilities dining-room, sitting-room, TV room, table-tennis room; terrace, garden; sauna
Credit Cards not accepted
Children very welcome
Disabled easy access via side entrance and ground floor
Pets accepted
Closed end Oct to mid-Dec; after Easter to end May
Languages English, some French
Proprietors Walcher family

Steiermark

Restaurant with rooms, Riegersburg

Gasthof Fink

Riegersburg Castle has to be one of the world's most imposing fortresses, sitting on a granite ridge, scowling over the Styrian countryside. What a grim contrast it makes with the genuine jollity of the Fink family inn at the foot of the crag. The solid, white rectangular hotel with its green shutters and decorated walls also has panoramic views, especially from the restaurant where Gottfried Fink (and now his sons) have a growing reputation. Our inspector tucked into 'an excellent lunch of boiled beef salad, dressed with pumpkin-seed oil'.

Don't, however, expect fancy comforts. The Finks are very down-to-earth. Terracotta tiled floors in the entrance lead to the open-plan café, bar and sitting area. The *Stüberl*, a smaller dining-room with bench seats, cherry-wood veneer furniture and panelled ceiling is unashamedly rural. Some of the bedrooms are still rather dark; those remodelled in 1989 are much lighter, with white walls and stripped-pine furniture. Outside, walnut and chestnut trees shade the terrace where parents sip the Styrian wines, children enjoy home-made ice cream, and all tuck into the barbecue, accompanied by music.

Nearby castle with Witches' Museum, birds of prey observatory.

8333 Riegersburg 29
Tel (03153) 216
Fax (03153) 7357
Location on hilltop, below castle; own car parking
Meals breakfast, lunch, dinner, snacks
Prices rooms AS270-850 with breakfast; DB&B from AS390; reductions for children; meals from AS120
Rooms 26 double, 6 single; all have bath or shower, central heating, TV, hairdrier, radio; some have phone
Facilities 5 dining-rooms, sitting-room, bar, billiard room; terrace
Credit Cards DC, MC, V
Children very welcome
Disabled not suitable
Pets accepted
Closed 3 weeks Nov; 2 weeks Feb
Languages English, French
Proprietors Fink family

Steiermark

Castle hotel, Sebersdorf

Schlosshotel Obermayerhofen

'The honeymoon suite would not be beneath the dignity of Elizabeth Taylor' was our inspector's verdict. It was meant as a compliment, for he reckoned this hilltop hotel was 'the last word in luxury'.

Bedrooms are named for noble Austrian families and all are on a grand scale. Plain colours such as cream, butter-yellow and apricot provide the background for antiques and Persian carpets. Some have four-poster beds, in others swathes of fabric are draped from a coronet above the headboard. Even the bathrooms are generous in size, with potted plants, huge towels, and the latest in fittings, including some whirlpool baths.

A hotel only since 1986, the estate has been in the family of Count Kottulinsky since 1777. Like so many castles in Austria, its plain exterior contrasts with the Renaissance arcades and staircases of the inner courtyard. Indoors, chandeliers glitter, parquet floors shine with polish, and huge windows let in plenty of light. In the ceremonial hall, an 18thC fresco depicts a fanciful jungle scene, complete with palm trees and growling leopard. The private chapel may be used for weddings.

Nearby castles; wildlife park; Stift Vorau.

8272 Sebersdorf
Tel (03333) 2503
Fax (03333) 250350
Location on low hill, near Vienna-Graz motorway; own car parking
Meals breakfast, lunch, dinner
Prices AS1440-2800 with breakfast; reductions for children; meals from AS200
Rooms 20 double; all have bath or shower, central heating, phone, TV, minibar, hairdrier, radio

Facilities dining-room, sitting-room, bar, billiard room; terrace; beauty salon, sauna
Credit Cards AE, DC, MC, V
Children accepted but not ideal
Disabled not suitable
Pets not accepted
Closed early Jan to end Feb
Languages English, French, Italian
Proprietor Graf Kottulinsky

Steiermark

Castle hotel, St. Oswald

Schloss Plankenwarth

Want to sleep where the Empress Maria Theresa slept? That room is part of a tower suite with views in all directions across the hills and valleys of Styria. There is even a red carpet in the bathroom, where the cast-iron bath has gilded taps. Other rooms are equally dramatic. The Abbé Suite is next to the chapel where the family confessor had his quarters; the Comtesse Suite has 18thC French-style green and white fabric on the walls; and the Ferdinand Room has a four-poster bed with sheer, white drapery. Our inspector was ready to settle in for 11 days, in order to try each one in succession.

The castle is reached by a steep lane that winds up above the village. What you see now is mainly 17thC, although the fortress dates back 600 years and includes features like the painted ceiling in the Renaissance Hall. The Waisocher family took over in 1981 and have restored it carefully. Frau Waisocher was an antiques dealer so furnishings are generally genuine baroque and Biedermeier pieces. Even the few modern beds fit in. There is a children's play area near the discreetly-landscaped swimming-pool. 'Truly striking; for sybarites with perfect taste.'

Nearby Graz; Lipizzaner Stud farm; caves at Semriach.

8113 St Oswald bei Graz
Tel (03123) 2838
Fax (03123) 283818
Location above village on a bluff; ample car parking, 7 under cover
Meals breakfast
Prices rooms AS1000-2000 with breakfast; reductions for children
Rooms 11 double; all have bath or shower, central heating, phone, TV, minibar, hairdrier, radio

Facilities breakfast-room, 3 sitting-rooms, billiard room; terrace, garden, outdoor swimming-pool
Credit Cards AE, DC, MC, V
Children welcome
Disabled not suitable
Pets accepted
Closed Nov to Easter
Languages English, French, Italian
Proprietors Waisocher family

Steiermark

❊ **Rural hotel, Turnau** ❊

Frühstückspension Kirchleiten

'Like being mothered and pampered by a favourite aunt in the country' was our inspector's reaction to the welcome extended by Irmgard Knapp in her 'enchanting village house, with verandahs covered in different varieties of geraniums.' Her husband, Bernhardt, is one of a long line of master carpenters, which explains the lovingly-carved staircase and the distinctive light-and-dark pine panelling in the dining-room. The house dates back to 1750 when it was built as a *Bauernhof* (farmhouse) with the usual 2 cows, some pigs and chickens. Since 1954, the Knapp family have expanded and improved it, all with their own hands. Even the two life-sized straw men on the stairway were made by Frau Knapp for a local carnival 20 years ago.

Our inspector was particularly taken with the rooms in the old house, which have wood-panelling and small square windows; many also have balconies. At the very top are small, cosy rooms 'like a dolls' house.' The new suites, on the other hand, have whitewashed walls and furniture of light-coloured pine with peasant floral decoration. Views are across the valley or over the garden with fruit trees and the village church behind.

Nearby riding school; winter sports; hang-gliding.

8625 Turnau 34
Tel (03863) 2234
Location in heart of entrancing village in valley; own car parking
Meals breakfast, lunch, dinner, snacks
Prices rooms AS180-400 with breakfast; reductions for children; meals from AS75
Rooms 10 double, 5 single; all have bath or shower, central heating, phone, TV, minibar, hairdrier

Facilities dining-room, sitting-room, bar; terrace
Credit Cards not accepted
Children very welcome
Disabled not suitable
Pets accepted
Closed Nov to mid-Dec
Languages English, French
Proprietors Knapp family

Steiermark

Restaurant with rooms, Weiz

Romantik Modernshof

The food is the main draw here. 'Refined Styrian' could mean a summer dinner of asparagus roulade and shrimp with noodles followed by a strawberry and wine sorbet. 'Excellent' was our inspector's verdict on his carefully-prepared meal, partnered by a local Traminer and eaten to the strains of Mozart's *Don Giovanni* enjoying his last meal. Our man was glad it was not his, since breakfast was another meal to be thoroughly enjoyed. The only drawback is the curved staircase that descends into the dining-room; with people going up and down, any chance of an intimate dinner is lost.

The hotel was built in 1977 on the site of an old farmhouse. Tucked away in the hills and surrounded by orchards, it is 'an island of green'. An attractive seating area behind the arched windows along the front is a pleasant place for coffee or before-dinner drinks. At the back, a yellow awning shades the terrace which looks out on the large swimming-pool. Our inspector gave his bedroom a 'comfortable' rating for the modern furniture and prints by naive artists on the walls; he was less enthusiastic about the garish orange tiles in the bathroom.

Nearby riding; Raabklamm nature reserve; gliding.

8160 Weiz, Büchl 32
Tel (03172) 3747
Fax (03172) 37472
Location landscaped hotel in Styrian hills; ample car parking
Meals breakfast, lunch, dinner, snacks
Prices rooms AS950-1500 with breakfast; DB&B from AS1400; meals from AS450
Rooms 8 double; all have bath or shower, central heating, phone, TV, hairdrier, radio

Facilities 2 dining-rooms, sitting-room, bar; terrace, garden; sauna, outdoor swimming-pool
Credit Cards AE, DC, MC, V
Children accepted but not suitable
Disabled not suitable
Pets accepted
Closed Jan 10 to end March
Languages English, French, Italian, Spanish
Proprietors Mayer family

Steiermark

❊ Village inn, Aich ❊

Gasthof Bärenwirt

A picture of the God of Wine greets guests just inside the main entrance of this 16thC tavern. The Pilz family are proud of their food. Rooms are plain but comfortable. Skiing on Hauser Kaibling is 5 minutes away by car. Golf nearby.

■ 8966 Aich-Assach **Tel** (03686) 4303 **Fax** (03686) 430345 **Meals** breakfast, lunch, dinner, snacks **Prices** rooms AS300-700 with breakfast; meals from AS100 **Rooms** 26, all with bath or shower, central heating, phone **Credit cards** not accepted **Closed** Oct, Mar **Languages** English

---

Village inn, Aigen im Ennstal

Gasthof Putterersee

Family-oriented, this 500-year old village inn sits on a quiet side-road, shaded by lime trees. 1960s dark wood is slowly being replaced by cheerful, pale pine inside. With large garden, fields and small lake, this is a safe, friendly spot for young children.

■ 8943 Aigen im Ennstal 13 **Tel** (03682) 22520 **Fax** (03682) 2252033 **Meals** breakfast, lunch, dinner, snacks **Prices** rooms AS350-700 with breakfast **Rooms** 12, with shower, central heating, phone, radio; 7 with shared facilities **Credit cards** not accepted **Closed** Nov **Languages** English, Italian

---

❊ Town hotel, Bad Aussee ❊

Villa Kristina

Everything about this 100-year old house is turn-of-the-century, from the furnishings to the dignified politeness of silver-haired owner, Friedl Raudaschl. Although regulars have been coming back for 30 years, newcomers are welcomed. Light cooking.

■ 8990 Bad Aussee **Tel** (06152) 2017 **Meals** breakfast, dinner, snacks **Prices** rooms AS420-1100 with breakfast **Rooms** 12, all with bath or shower, central heating, phone **Credit cards** AE, DC, MC, V **Closed** mid-Nov to mid-Dec **Languages** English, French, Italian, Spanish

---

❊ Family hotel, Bad Mitterndorf ❊

Hotel Kogler

The Koglers have been specializing in children's holidays in the Salzkammergut for 40 years. They have recently added a new indoor swimming-pool, sauna, solarium, as well as 2 tennis-courts. Nannies entertain children with walks, campfires.

■ 8983 Bad Mitterndorf **Tel** (06153) 23250 **Fax** (06153) 3107 **Meals** breakfast, lunch, dinner, snacks **Prices** rooms DB&B for 2, AS450-750 **Rooms** 31, all with bath or shower, central heating, phone, TV **Credit cards** not accepted **Closed** Nov to mid-Dec; 2 weeks after Easter **Languages** English

Steiermark

❋ Farmhouse hotel, Gröbming ❋

Gasthof Reisslerhof

Surrounded by fields, with a working farm and riding school next door, this is an ideal spot for family holidays. Rooms are modern, with space for both parents and children. Rural informality. Only 10 minutes from ski-slopes.

■ 8962 Gröbming-Mitterberg **Tel** (03685) 22364 **Fax** (03685) 2236410 **Meals** breakfast, lunch, dinner, snacks **Prices** rooms AS350-700 with breakfast; meals from AS120 **Rooms** 25, all with bath and shower, central heating, phone **Credit cards** not accepted **Closed** Nov **Languages** English, French, some Italian

---

Lakeside guest-house, Grundlsee

Gasthof Ladner

On the shores of the Grundlsee lake, near the cable-car up to the Appelhaus, this simple inn is ideal for walkers who want an inexpensive base to explore the Totes Gebirge mountains behind. Christine Grill provides uncomplicated home-cooking.

■ 8993 Grundlsee, Gössl 1 **Tel** (06152) 8211 **Meals** breakfast, lunch, dinner, snacks **Prices** rooms AS230-700 with breakfast; meals from AS100 **Rooms** 6, all with bath or shower **Credit cards** not accepted **Closed** Nov to March **Languages** English

---

Restaurant with rooms, Judenburg

Rasthaus Grünhübl

The unattractive exterior hides an art deco-style gem of a bar, complete with illuminated glass panels. Near the Österreichring motor-racing circuit, this busy wayside inn is a favourite with cyclists following the River Mur. Honest Styrian cooking.

■ 8750 Judenburg, Burggasse 132 **Tel** (03572) 2437 **Fax** (03572) 45558 **Meals** breakfast, lunch, dinner, snacks **Prices** rooms AS300-900 with breakfast **Rooms** 14, all with shower, central heating, phone, TV, minibar, radio **Credit cards** AE, DC, MC, V **Closed** 1 week Feb **Languages** English, French, Italian, Czech

---

❋ Country hotel, Kitzeck ❋

Pension Steirerland

Although the building is a standard, modern chalet, it boasts a striking hill-top position, with views to the Slovenian Alps and a huge, covered terrace. Meals are delicious, Styrian-style, with unusual wine soups. Ruth Stelzer is a charming hostess.

■ 8442 Kitzeck, Höch am Demmerkogel **Tel** (03456) 328 **Meals** breakfast, lunch, dinner, snacks **Prices** rooms AS300-800 with breakfast; meals from AS150 **Rooms** 10, all with bath and shower, central heating, phone, TV, radio **Credit cards** not accepted **Closed** Jan, Feb **Languages** English, French

Steiermark

❄ Country guest-house, Krakauebene ❄

Haus Schaller

Children enjoy playing with the chickens and goats; cross-country skiers stop at local farmhouses for a *Schnaps;* families go for sleigh-rides. The Schnedlitz's simple hotel is a place to relax, high in the Tauern range. Own tennis-court.

■ 8854 Krakauebene 55, Klausen **Tel** (03535) 334 **Meals** breakfast, lunch, dinner, snacks **Prices** rooms AS180-450 with breakfast; meals from AS100 **Rooms** 13, all with bath or shower, central heating **Credit cards** not accepted **Closed** Nov to mid-Dec; May **Languages** English

---

❄ Farmhouse inn, Krieglach ❄

Annerlbauerhof

Stuffed animals and open fires greet guests. Upstairs, old-fashioned Alpine-style bedrooms and split-level apartments are rather dark. Honest country cooking. Floodlit ski trails on the doorstep. Ideal for low-cost, unpretentious outdoor holidays.

■ 8670 Krieglach, Malleisten 15 **Tel** (03855) 2228 **Meals** breakfast, lunch, dinner, snacks **Prices** rooms AS275-550 with breakfast **Rooms** 13, all with bath or shower; TV on request **Credit cards** not accepted **Closed** mid-Oct to mid-Nov; Easter **Languages** German only

---

❄ Bed-and-breakfast hotel, Mariazell ❄

Mariazellerhof

Mariazell is Austria's main pilgrimage destination. The Pirker family's hotel is only 200 metres west of the 14thC basilica. Built in 1969, it is modern, but also cheerful and comfortable. Ski-school and Bürgeralpe slopes within walking distance.

■ 8630 Mariazell **Tel** (03882) 2179 **Fax** (03882) 217951 **Meals** breakfast **Prices** rooms AS350-950 with breakfast **Rooms** 14, all with bath or shower, central heating, phone, TV **Credit cards** DC, MC **Closed** never **Languages** English

---

❄ Converted Alpine hut, Mühlen ❄

Tonnerhütte und Gästehaus

Our intrepid inspector drove up "a vertical, unmetalled road to a mountain hut at the end of the world". Fabulous views from Jakobsberg across the valley. Rustic rooms. Some skiing, nearby lift, no crowds. Perfect for getting back to nature. Inexpensive.

■ 8822 Mühlen, Jakobsberg 2 **Tel** (03584) 3250 **Meals** breakfast, lunch, dinner, snacks **Prices** rooms AS200-560 with breakfast **Rooms** 5, with shower; 5, with wash-basins **Credit cards** not accepted **Closed** Nov; 3 weeks after Easter **Languages** English, Italian

Steiermark

❁ Family hotel, Murau ❁

Murauer Gasthof-Hotel Lercher

In an old town in Western Styria, this traditional inn manages to be all things to all guests. There is a gourmet candle-light dinner on the first Saturday of the month, a children's *Stammtisch,* wine-tasting, musical evenings. Skiing nearby.

■ 8850 Murau, Schwarzenbergstr 10 **Tel** (03532) 2431 **Fax** (03532) 3694 **Meals** breakfast, lunch, dinner, snacks **Prices** rooms AS425-1000 with breakfast; meals from AS100 **Rooms** 26, all with bath or shower, central heating, phone, TV **Credit cards** MC **Closed** never **Languages** English, French

❁ Country inn, Mürzsteg ❁

Gasthof-Pension Schönauer

Owner Meta Schönauer pops up to cook for the President of Austria when he is on holiday at the Jagdschloss above. Although the Treaty of Macedonia was signed here by the Russian tsar and the Austro-Hungarian emperor, this inn is refreshingly simple.

■ 8693 Mürzsteg **Tel** (03859) 2214 **Meals** breakfast, lunch, dinner, snacks **Prices** rooms AS240-480 with breakfast **Rooms** 9, all with bath or shower, central heating **Credit cards** not accepted **Closed** mid-Oct to mid-Nov **Languages** German only

❁ Mountain hotel, near Obdach ❁

Judenburger Hütte

Approaching this remote mountain retreat, deer leap across the steep road through the woods. The tennis-courts are the highest in Styria (1420 m) and the Sauers own 2 ski-lifts. Cross-country skiing from the door. Large swimming-pools but few frills.

■ 8742 St. Wolfgang am Zirbitz, Obdach **Tel** (03578) 8202 **Meals** breakfast, lunch, dinner, snacks **Prices** rooms AS370-660 with breakfast **Rooms** 16, all with bath or shower, central heating **Credit cards** not accepted **Closed** 3 weeks Nov; 3 weeks April **Languages** English, French, Italian

Village inn, Obdach

Groggerhof

On the main street of Obdach, this 360-year old inn has a growing reputation for its food thanks to Éva Ederer-Grogger. Visitors and locals enjoy her authentic Styrian cooking, with as many as a dozen wines available by the glass.

■ 8742 Obdach, Hauptplatz **Tel** (03578) 2201 **Fax** (03578) 2660 **Meals** breakfast, lunch, dinner, snacks **Prices** rooms AS290-650 with breakfast **Rooms** 15, all with bath or shower, central heating, phone, TV **Credit cards** not accepted **Closed** never; restaurant only, Tues **Languages** English

Steiermark

Bakery with rooms, Puch bei Weiz

Landgasthof Eitljörg

The mouth-watering scent of fresh baking greets guests to this 100-year old hotel in the heart of Styria's apple-orchards. Bedrooms in the older building are nicely old-fashioned. Special apple diets, apple *Schnaps*, apple *Sekt*.

■ 8182 Puch bei Weiz **Tel** (03177) 2204 **Fax** (03177) 3225 **Meals** breakfast, lunch, dinner, snacks **Prices** rooms AS300-800 with breakfast; meals from AS100 **Rooms** 14, all with bath or shower, central heating; TV on request **Credit cards** MC **Closed** Nov or Jan **Languages** English, French

Old inn, St Gallen

Gasthof Hensle

This solid cream-and-brown inn has faced the square with its statue of John of Nepomuk for centuries. Although the *Stüberl* which doubles as the breakfast room has beams dated 1509, the bedrooms are modern and functional. A useful overnight stop.

■ 8933 St Gallen 43 **Tel** (03632) 7171 **Fax** (03632) 717123 **Meals** breakfast, lunch, dinner, snacks **Prices** rooms AS300-800 with breakfast **Rooms** 16, all with bath or shower, central heating, phone, TV, radio **Credit cards** AE, DC, MC **Closed** 1 week Oct; restaurant only, Wed **Languages** English

❊ Modern hotel, Stadl an der Mur ❊

Murtalerhof

Bright, new hotel; rather lacking in character. However, Johann Lassacher prepares authentic Styrian dishes, much appreciated by rafting enthusiasts who hurtle down the Mur river. Cavernous dining-room; plain bedrooms. Skiing at Kreischberg, 5 km.

■ 8862 Stadl an der Mur, Steindorf 11 **Tel** (03534) 2237 **Fax** (0316) 271973 **Meals** breakfast, lunch, dinner, snacks **Prices** rooms AS280-640 with breakfast; meals from AS150 **Rooms** 23, all with bath or shower, central heating, phone, TV, hairdrier **Credit cards** MC, V **Closed** never **Languages** English, French, Italian

❊ Medieval inn, near Stein/Enns ❊

Gasthof 'Zum Gamsjäger'

This 13thC inn has been carefully modernized, so some Gothic features, such as ceilings, survive. A useful base to explore the breathtaking Sölk pass, the Sölktaler nature reserve. Pale pinks, blues, pine-wood in bedrooms.

■ 8961 Stein/Enns, St Nikolai 127 **Tel** (03689) 210 **Meals** breakfast, lunch, dinner, snacks **Prices** rooms AS210-460 with breakfast, meals from AS80 **Rooms** 17, all with bath or shower, central heating, radio **Credit cards** not accepted **Closed** 2 weeks in Nov **Languages** German only

Index of hotel names

In this index, hotels are arranged in order of the most distinctive part of their name; in many cases, other parts of the name are also given after the main part, but very common prefixes such as 'Hotel', 'Gasthof' and 'Das' are omitted. Where a hotel's name begins with Schloss or Schlosshotel, it will normally be indexed under the word that follows. Hotels covered in the several Area introductions are not indexed.

Index of hotel names

Index of hotel names

Index of hotel names

Index of hotel locations

In this index, hotels are arranged by the name of city, town or village they are in or near. Where a hotel is located in a very small place, it may be indexed under a nearby place which is more easily found on maps. Hotels in well-known resort areas such as Attersee or Faakersee are listed under the lake in general, then the specific village.

Index of hotel locations

Index of hotel locations

Index of hotel locations

Index of hotel locations

Near Salzburg For visitors who prefer to stay near the city,
rather than in it, we list the towns where we have recommended
hotels within about 80 km/1 hour's drive of Salzburg. Most are
in Salzburgerland, listed between pages 62 and 84:

Abtenau, Altenmarkt, Dorfgastein, Filzmoos, Fuschl am See,
Goldegg, Hallein, Leogang, Mattsee, Oberalm, St Gilgen,
Strasswalchen, Wagrain and Werfen. There are three towns in
Oberösterreich, listed between pages 86 and 102. In Styria,
Altaussee (pages 163/164) is 80 km from Salzburg.

Near Vienna For visitors who prefer to stay near the capital,
rather than in it, we list the towns where we have recommended
hotels within about 80 km/1 hour's drive of Vienna. Some are in
Niederösterreich, listed between pages 104 and 122:

Baden, Dürnstein, Klein-Wien, Klosterneuberg, Krems,
Laaben, Mautern, Mayerling, Payerbach, Puchberg am
Schneeberg, Tullnerbach and Weissenkirchen.

The rest are in Burgenland, listed between pages 135 and 140:

Eisenstadt, Gols, Mörbisch, Neusiedl and Purbach.

Reporting to the guides

Please write and tell us about your experiences of small hotels, guest-houses and inns, whether good or bad, whether listed in this edition or not. As well as hotels in Austria, we are interested in charming small hotels in: Britain, Ireland, Italy, France, Spain, Portugal, Germany, Switzerland and other European countries, as well as the east and west coasts of the United States.

The address to write to is:

The Editors,
Austria,
Charming Small Hotel Guides,
Duncan Petersen Publishing Ltd,
54 Milson Road,
London, W14 0LB,
England.

Checklist
Please use a separate sheet of paper for each report; include your name, address and telephone number on each sheet.
  Your reports are particularly welcome if they are typed and organized under the following headings:

Name of establishment
Town or village
Full address and post code
Telephone number
Time and duration of visit
The building and setting
Public rooms
Bedrooms and bathrooms
Standards of maintenance, housekeeping
Standards of comfort and decoration
Atmosphere, welcome and service
Food
Value for money

We assume that in writing you have no objection to your views being published unpaid, either verbatim or in an edited version. Names of major outside contributors are acknowledged in the guide, at the editor's discretion.